Gold on the Diamond

Sacramento's Great Baseball Players 1886 to 1976

Tony Freitas (Author's Collection)

on the Diamond

Sacramento's Great Baseball Players
1886 to 1976

Alan O'Connor

To Jerry & Rita —
Great Solons
fans.

Alan O'Connor

BIGTOMATOPRESS

*This book is dedicated
to my all-time all-sports stars,
Megan and Mike.*

Library of Congress Cataloging-in-Publication Data
O'Connor, Alan.
Gold on the Diamond: Sacramento's Great Baseball Players
1886 to 1976 / Alan O'Connor. 1st ed.
p. cm.
Includes index.
ISBN-13: 978-0-9791233-0-6
ISBN-10:0-9791233-0-5
1. Baseball — California — Sacramento — History.
2. Pacific Coast League — History.
3. Baseball players — California — Sacramento — Biography.
GV865.A1 2008
796.357 2008

Big Tomato Press
1126 2nd Street, Sacramento, California 95814
www.bigtomatopress.com

CONTENTS

1947 Solons road jersey (Author's Collection)

ACKNOWLEDGMENTS

This book was inspired by the works of John Spalding. His *Always on Sunday* and *Sacramento Senators and Solons* books provided the background that enabled me to embark on this project. Also, the biographical structure in this book pays tribute to Spalding's book, *100 PCL Stars Who Made it to the Majors*. I encourage you to read all of Spalding's baseball books.

I want to thank Fran Pendleton for her pioneering work in Sacramento baseball of the 19th century. Her work made mine easier, and her encouragement on this book kept me going.

Carlos Bauer's Pacific Coast League Cyclopedia was an invaluable tool. Ray Nemec provided a wealth of statistical data. Mike McCann's website, www.geocities.com/big_bunko, helped me figure out the forgotten names of teams from long ago. Thanks also to the knowledgeable, reliable, helpful and friendly staff members in the Sacramento Room of the Sacramento Public Library's Central Branch on I Street, and the Sacramento Archives and Museum Collection Center (SAMCC). Bill Gaylord and Mark Macrae helped bring this book into a readable state.

Mark Macrae and Doug McWilliams have spent much time over several years mentoring me in my search for information and for images of Sacramento baseball in the California and Pacific Coast leagues.

I also want to thank Bill Shubb for all his assistance and encouragement, and for providing the Solons website for everyone's enjoyment. It can be found at sacramentosolons.com.

My thanks also to Lee Susman for so generously sharing his inspired cartoons of the Solons Dome in action, and for allowing me to use them in this book.

And thanks to Walt Fitzpatrick are in order for his technical assistance and coaching in the production of this book.

I also want to thank the following individuals for their help and support: Tim Armstrong, Marlene Arts, Cuno Barragan, Dick Beverage, Carrolla Blue-bar, Vicky Bordagaray, Becky Carruthers, Kim Cherwin, Carol Cowden, Ron Crumb, Doug Dahl, Ralpha Pearl Daniels, Dr. Roger Daniels, Fred David, David Dow, Peter Doyle, Mike Duncan, Kristin Elder, Claire Ellis, Dave Eskinazi, Ed Fitz Gerald, Walt Fitzpatrick, Zak Ford, Barbara Foskett, Patti Funk, Stan Gilliam, John Gonzales, Mary Helmich, Carson Hendricks, Jim Henley, Gene Itogawa, Pat Johnson, Sam Kanelos, Jack Keefe, Robert Keefe, Michael Kennedy, Greg King, Ron King, Dave Lawrence, Dylan MacDonald, Walter McCoy, Bill McNulty, Byron Milstead, John Moist, Kevin Morse, Rich Myers, Sheila Baer Neal, Michael O'Connor, Roger Osenbaugh, Marguerite Pintar, Craig Rader, Janet Reaves, Miles Richmond, Ray Saracini, Kevin Schanz, Bryan Shadden, John Shaw, Mike Sheely, Neill Sheridan, Gus Stathos, Tom Tolley, Pat Turse, Christina Voss, Bud Watkins, Wally Westlake, Jeri Hughes Wingfield, Melinda Wiley-Dahl, Kelly Williams, Lee Winter, and Ken Wollenberg.

Jo Jo White's 1945 Solons hat (Author's Collection)

Pre WWI Senators catcher's mask (Author's Collection)

FOREWORD

There are enough volumes based on the old Pacific Coast League to fill a good-sized bookcase. That's the PCL composed of just eight teams, all in West Coast cities (with a stretch for a short period into Utah), as contrasted with today's 16-club, four-division circuit stretching from coast to coast. Those books are all filled with numbers, statistical figures that give true fans something to talk about during the Hot Stove League season, when the players aren't on the field. Most of the names are tied to individuals — players or managers — but that's all they are, just names. Now Alan O'Connor has come along to flesh out those skeletal names and bring some of those men back to life, the most interesting, the most unusual, the most memorable for one reason or another, who played for or managed the Sacramento Senators/Solons. It's a book that fills a need — a niche need, perhaps, but still a real need. It's a volume any fan of earlier times will find enjoyable. Like that fellow peddling clothing on TV, I guarantee it.

— Stan Gilliam, Sacramento, 2006

1955 Solons team signed ball (Author's Collection)

INTRODUCTION

I've always been enthusiastic about baseball and about Sacramento history, and this book is the result. It's my attempt to put a face on many of the Sacramento-area residents who played on professional baseball teams here from 1886 through the mid-1970s. My goal in writing was to share my interest and research, and at the same time, preserve a record of the players, the teams and a little bit about the way baseball was played here for 121 years.

I grew up in Sacramento and was lucky enough to know some Solons players and live down the block or around the corner from others. I called this book *Gold on the Diamond* because I wanted to bring front and center those great players from the past who represented River City baseball well before 2000 when the excitement of the River Cats arrived at Raley Field. Just like today's River Cats, the Sacramento Solons were PCL champions in their time.

Except for the 1980s and '90s, professional baseball has been a major part of life in Sacramento since the 1880s. There are still many of us who remember turning in a foul ball and getting a free ticket into Edmonds Field. A lot of old-time Sacramentans recall going to Solons games when the park was called Cardinal Field. Some remember the heroics of Tony Freitas, especially his major role in winning the 1942 PCL Championship. I even have a couple of friends who remember games when the park was called Moreing Field. It wasn't all that long ago that Sacramento fans had their favorite players: "Demon" Doyle, Jay Hughes, "Duster" Mails, Ray French, Earl McNeely, Tony Freitas, "Manny" Salvo, Jo Jo White, Ed Fitz Gerald, Joe Marty, Wally

Westlake, Roger Osenbaugh, "Bud" Watkins, Richie Myers, Al Heist, "Cuno" Barragan and "Bill" McNulty.

Most of the players I have written about were born in or around Sacramento or grew up here. Others settled down and raised their families in Sacramento after their professional playing days were behind them. I've presented the players in the order that they first appeared on a Sacramento team, that way the biographies form an easy-to-follow timeline of our baseball history. I've also included a gallery of players, coaches and business owners — some famous, others infamous — who left their indelible marks on our historic record.

I am always looking for new information about Sacramento's great baseball history, and I hope to create follow-up editions to this book. If you can add to, clarify or shed light on the historic data that has been presented here, please contact me. If you know something about Sacramento's teams or players you'd like to share or have old photos or ephemera that will add to the body of knowledge about baseball before the River Cats, I'd welcome the chance to hear your stories. Just as I hope you will enjoy this book, you will find me an eager listener.

Please write me at P. O. Box 188284, Sacramento, Calif., 95818 or email me at alanoconnor@sbcglobal.net

Now, let's play ball.

1889 Altas Player woodcut
(Sacramento Bee, Author's Collection)

Teens Senators catcher's mitt
(Author's Collection)

Senators cap, teens era (Author's Collection)

A SUMMARY OF BASEBALL HISTORY IN SACRAMENTO

Baseball has been played in Northern California, especially in the Sacramento area, since the days of the Gold Rush. Local ball clubs existed at both the recreational and "semi-pro" levels. The first written record of baseball in Sacramento was in the November 1859 *Daily Union*. It indicated a local base ball club (in general, before World War I, baseball was written as two words) had been organized using "New York rules." According to Sacramento historian Frances Pendleton, the first "finished" game in California was in Sacramento in 1860 at the California State Fair Base Ball Tournament. The game was between the Eagles of San Francisco and the Sacramento Club. San Francisco won the game and was awarded a "Silver Ball" trophy.

In September 1869, a local team was assembled to play the visiting professional Cincinnati Red Stockings (generally recognized as the first professional baseball team in America), with Cincinnati winning 50–6. In 1883 the first professional league in the state, the California League, was established with five teams from San Francisco and Oakland. The California League was expanded to include a Sacramento team, the Sacramento Altas, in 1886.

SACRAMENTO

SELNA

ROXBURG, CATCHER.

NEWBERT

BASE BALL CLUB.

HUGHES.

GLEASON, MANAGER.

1889.

ROBERTS.

ZEIGLER, PITCHER.

GAGUS, CAPT.

KNELL, PITCHER.

VEACH.

GOODENOUGH.

Abell & Priest

BANCROFT'S
HISTORY BUILD
723 MARKET ST.

1889.

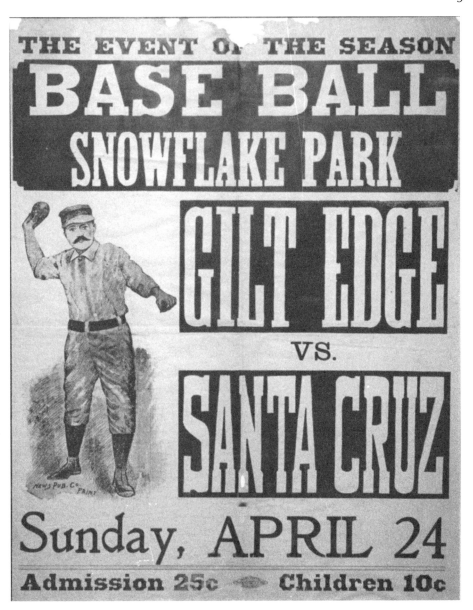

Left: Abell and Priest were photographers based in San Francisco. This 1889
photo features the Sacramento Base Ball Club players (clockwise from top
left) Selna; Roxburg, Catcher; Newbert; Roberts; Knell, pitcher; Goodenough;
Gagus, Captain; Veach; Zeigler, pitcher; and manager Gleason in the center.
Above: 1898 Poster (Author's Collection).

1898 Gilt Edge Team. The word Ruhstaller, for the brewery that made Gilt Edge beer, is embroidered on their sweaters (Author's Collection).

OFFICIAL SCORE CARD

CALIFORNIA STATE LEAGUE

MAY 26th and 27th

RUHSTALLER'S GILT EDGE
AND BUFFALO NEW BREW
ON DRAUGHT

A. B. & T. W. SCHAAP
PROPRIETORS

DAD AND TOM

The Pacific

Choicest Wines, Liquors and Cigars

614 J STREET...

GO TO THE——

Capital News Co.

702 K STREET, Opp. Postoffice

All Sporting Papers
A Full Line of Stationery

A Specialty--10c Novels Circulating Library

GO TO THE POPULAR
GILT EDGE SALOON
——FOR A FINE——
Glass of Beer or Porter,
1014 J STREET,
JACOB GRUHLER, Prop.

1900 Program (Author's Collection).

DECADE HIGHLIGHTS

1880s

In 1886, the Sacramento Altas joined the California League and played against teams from the San Francisco Bay Area. The term "Alta" refers to Northern California. The Altas lost their opening game 4-3 to the San Francisco Pioneers, but eventually placed a respectable second in a five-team league with a 17-14 record. The other teams were the Oakland Greenhood and Morans, the San Francisco Haverlys, the San Francisco Pioneers and the San Francisco Stars. Sacramento's George Borchers led all California League pitchers with a 4-1 record, and Russ Flint came in second in the league in batting with a .273 average (the top batter hit .274).

The Altas played at Agriculture Park, which was in the area between 20th and 23rd streets and E and H streets, and later at Snowflake Park, which was between 28th and 30th streets and R and S streets.

In 1887 the Altas finished in third place with a 19–19 record, and in 1888 jumped to a semi-pro league so they could have more home games and attempt to generate more revenue.

Delivery slip for Rushstaller's Gilt Edge Beer (Author's Collection).

OPENING DAY 1903 SACRAMENTO SENATORS

Sacramento Senators on Opening Day in 1903, traveling by the State House Hotel in downtown Sacramento, where single rooms were 50 cents and meals were 25 cents, on their way to Oak Park for the first ever PCL game (Doug McWilliams Collection).

1903 Sacramento player (Author's Collection).

1911 Senators team photo (Author's Collection).

But the grass was not greener in the new league, and in 1889 the Altas returned to the California League and moved into Snowflake Park. Unfortunately they finished last in what was then a four-team league.

1890s

In 1890 the team, now called the Senators, improved their level of play and they produced a second-place finish with a 79–58 record. They finished the season tied with the San Francisco team, but lost the playoff series to them. Sacramento's George Harper led the league in pitching with a 41-26 record.

In 1891 the Senators finished in third place with a 17-23 record. In 1892 Sacramento did not field a team, but in 1893, the Senators finished last in the league with an 8-14 record.

From 1894 to 1897, The California League and the Sacramento Senators did not exist, each a likely casualty of The Panic of 1893, an economic depression caused by a run on the country's gold supply.

In 1898 Ruhstaller's Brewery sponsored a new Sacramento team, naming it the Gilt Edge after one of its beers. The team, however, was commonly called the Brewers. They were California League champions in 1898 with a 49-27 record. Brewer Charles "Demon" Doyle led all pitchers in the league with a 10-5 record. The Brewers repeated their league-champion feat in 1899, and again "Demon" Doyle was the league's top pitcher with a 28-11 record. Gilt Edge Ervin Harvey was the 1899 batting champ with a .350 average.

1900s

In 1900 the Gilt Edge posted a 50-35 record and won the California League championship for the third straight time — a three-peat! Jay Hughes led the league in pitching with a 23-9 record.

In 1901 Sacramento's team became the Senators, and they finished third in the four-team league. Ernest Courtney led the league in batting with a .309 average. "Demon" Doyle went 20-12.

In 1902 the Senators finished last. Some say Elmer Stricklin, who pitched during the season, became the first spitball pitcher in the major leagues when he was with the Chicago White Sox.

A new era in baseball began on the West Coast in 1903. The Pacific Coast League (PCL) was formed and the first PCL game was played in Sacramento between the Senators and the Oakland Oaks. Sacramento won the game, 7-4. The Senators "Truck" Eagan led the league that year in home runs with 13. The Senators were sometimes called the "Blues" because of their blue uniforms.

In 1904, Sacramento left the PCL because attendance was down. The team moved to Tacoma, Wash., was renamed the Tacoma Tigers, and won the PCL championship.

In 1905 Sacramento did not have a team, but in 1906 a team known as the Senators in the six-team "outlaw" California State League (CSL), finished third in the league.

Some of the players had been on the 1903 PCL Senators team, including "Demon" Doyle and Charlie Graham. In 1907 the team finished second among the six teams, and Fred Brown led the league in pitching with a 24-6 record. In 1908 the Senators finished third in the league, which had grown to include eight teams. Joe Nealon led the league in batting with a .372 average, and Sacramento's Harry Hooper signed with the Boston Red Sox and went on to a Hall-of-Fame career.

Bill Rodgers (1918) and Art Griggs (1919) on Zee-Nut Candy cards. (Author's Collection).

A 1914 Charley Doyle cigar shop token showing Sacramento's game schedule with varous Pacific Coast League teams, The token reveals the unofficial name of the Wolves (after manager Harry Wolverton). Actual Size 1.5 inches. (Author's Collection)

Rare Moses Yellowhorse
(1924) Zee-Nut Candy card.
Yellowhorse was the first
Native American to play
for Sacramento. (Author's
Collection).

This 1914 pennant displays the Sacramento Senator's nickname: the
Wolves. Mark Macrae Collection).

In 1909 the Senators returned to sanctioned baseball as part of the PCL, and played at Oak Park (now called McClatchy Park) on Fifth Avenue between 33rd and 37th streets.

1910s

In 1910 the Senators moved to Buffalo Park on the southeast corner of what is now Riverside Boulevard and Broadway. This remained the site for all of Sacramento's teams through 1960. The new park, however, did not stimulate better baseball, and the Senators finished in last place.

The Senators had mediocre years from 1911 through 1914, although they did finish second in 1913. From 1913 through 1914 Harry Wolverton, who had managed the 1912 New York Yankees, managed the Senators. During this time the team was often called the "Wolves." It was also during the early teens that the Senators were nicknamed the Solons (another term for legislator) by sportswriters. Lefty Williams, later of the infamous Chicago "Black Sox," pitched for the Senators in 1914. The Senators left Sacramento in

Sacramento Senatora 1924 Opening Day at Moreing Field. (Author's Collection).

September 1914 to become the San Francisco Missions. Sacramento was without a team from 1915 to 1917. In 1915 the Missions moved to Salt Lake City, Utah, to become the Bees.

In 1918 Sacramento had a new Senators team stocked with many ballplayers from the defunct Portland, Ore., team. One of these players was Bill "Rawmeat" Rodgers who got his nickname from both his demeanor and eating preferences. He played second base and managed the Senators though 1921. Art Griggs led the league in batting with a .378 average, but the team managed to finish only fourth of six teams. In 1919 the Senators also produced a fourth-place finish in the eight-team league.

1920s

In 1920 Lew Moreing bought the Senators and remained owner through the 1933 season. Former Gilt Edge pitcher Charley "Demon" Doyle became team secretary in 1920. The 1920 season, however, was uneventful, and

The Wolves

In the early 20th century many teams used the last name of a star player or manager as the team nickname. Wilbert Robinson managed the Brooklyn Dodgers from 1914-31, and the team was nicknamed the "Robins." From 1902-11 Napoleon "Nap" Lajoie played for the Cleveland Indians, nicknamed as the "Naps." Senators team schedules and pennants bore the wolf head of the "Wolves" in tribute to manager Harry Wolverton.

SACRAMENTO
——BALL CLUB——

Pacific Coast League Games at Sacramento and Stockton for 1930

Top Row from Left to Right—Thomas, Coyle, Gillick, Philbin, Haze, Herrick, Brown, Hoag, Camilli, Flynn, Freitas, Steinbacker, Burke.
Center Row from Left to Right—Lew Moreing, Buddy Ryan, manager, Stoeven, Jones, Rohwer, Backer, Bryan, Hood, Osborne.
Bottom Row from Left to Right—Reeder, Keating, Downey, trainer, Koehler, McLaughlin, Wirts, Gould, French, Murphy.

Sacramento 1930 Team Photo. (Author's Collection).

the Senators finished seventh. In 1921 prospects improved when the Senators finished in second place. That ranking, and a complete remodel of Buffalo Park (renamed Moreing Field), brought renewed hopes to fans for 1922. The team, however, finished in last place.

In 1923, the Senators were back with a second-place finish. That same year, pitcher Moses Yellowhorse became the first Native American to play for Sacramento. The years 1924 through 1927 produced no better than a fourth-place finish. John "Buddy" Ryan, one of Sacramento's favorite players and managers, took over as a manager in 1924 and was a fixture until 1932.

One of the decade's bright spots came after the close of the 1927 season when barnstorming teams led by Babe Ruth and Lou Gehrig played at Moreing Field. To the delight of the crowd, each of the Yankees stars produced home runs.

The Senators had a banner year in 1928. They played great baseball all year long and won the second-half championship (the league championship was decided in a series played between the first- and second-half winners). They did lose the playoff to the first-half champion San Francisco Seals, and in 1929 slipped back into the second division (the lower half of the standings).

1930s

In the 1930s, the country was in an economic depression and Sacramento's baseball fortunes followed. In 1930 the Senators finished third out of eight teams in the PCL, with one highlight coming on June 10, when Sacramento hosted the Oakland Oaks in the first PCL night game. From 1931 through 1936, the highest the Senators climbed was third place.

In 1932 Kenso Nushida became the first Asian American to play for the team. After the 1933 season, various banks owned the Senators.

But 1936 ushered in a new beginning for Sacramento baseball. The team was purchased by the St. Louis Cardinals and became one of its top farm clubs. The name Solons had been used informally since before World War I, but it now became the official team name. Also the name of the ballpark was changed from Moreing Field to Cardinal Field.

The last three years of the 1930s were exciting for Solons' fans. In 1937 the team placed first in the regular season standings for the first time since 1900. The actual league championship, however, was decided by the Governor's Cup, a playoff of the top four teams. The Solons were eliminated in the first round. In both 1938 and 1939 the Solons won the Governor's Cup, but in those two years the championship was awarded to the season's first-place

1932 photo of Kenso Nushida
(Doug McWilliams Collection).

finisher. The post-season Governor's Cup provided entertainment for the fans and additional money for the teams and the players.

1940s

In 1940 the Solons slipped to fifth place, but in 1941 came back up to second.

In 1942 the Solons won the league championship with a 105-73 record. At the end of the season, down by four games with five to go, second-place Sacramento won five in a row over the first-place Los Angeles Angels. The last two games were a Sunday doubleheader at Cardinal Field, and the Solons beat the Angels in both games to take the championship. PCL Hall-

1937 Team Photo. (Author's Collection).

1942 Team Photo. (Author's Collection).

1942 Pacific Coast League Championship Ring. (Author's Collection).

1946 Team Photo. (Author's Collection).

Solons coach Dolph Camilli and manager Del Baker in 1949 (Author's Collection).

of-Fame pitcher Tony Freitas got the save in the first game and the win in the second! In 1943, however, the team was dismantled as the Cardinals downsized their farm system because of World War II, and the Solons plummeted to last place with the worst ever PCL record of 41-114.

After 1944, the Solons' association with the Cardinals ended, and the team was sold to a group of local businessmen called the Sacramento Baseball Association. Dick Edmonds, Sacramento Union sports editor, was instrumental in the formation of the group, which saved the Solons by keeping them in Sacramento.

In 1944, after a newspaper contest, Cardinal Field was re-named Doubleday Field, and the Solons finished fifth. They finished fifth again in 1945 and 1946. Edmonds died in 1945, and the field was re-named Edmonds Field in his honor. In 1947 the Solons finished seventh.

In 1948 the Solons finished last and had to play half the season on the road because Edmonds Field burned in July. By 1949, Edmonds Field had been rebuilt and an improved team moved up to third place.

1950s

In his book Sacramento Senators and Solons, John Spalding refers to the 1950s Solons as "bottom feeders." During this decade the Solons were truly not competitive — a major factor in their ultimate demise. During the 1950s, the Solons never climbed any higher than fourth place and finished last four times.

In 1950 two noteworthy changes occurred. The Solons broke the color

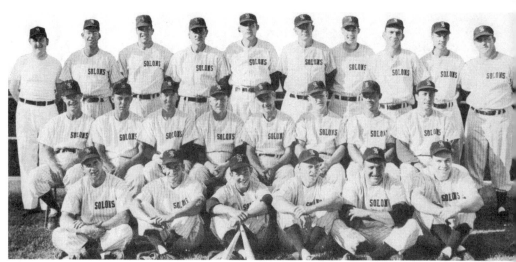

1953 Team Photo. (Author's Collection).

Walt McCoy (right) and Marvin Williams, 1950. (Author's Collection).

1959 Team Photo. (Author's Collection).

barrier with Marvin Williams at second base and Walter McCoy pitching. Both had previously played in the Negro Leagues — McCoy for the Chicago American Giants and Williams for the Philadelphia Stars. They came to the Solons together from a team in Venezuela. In spite of their talents, neither one ever played in the major leagues. Also in 1950, Tony Freitas, Sacramento's greatest pitcher, played his last game for the Solons, retiring with a 224-168 win-loss record.

From 1951 to 1952 Joe Gordon was one of the last player-managers in professional baseball. Gordon also was the Pacific Coast League's home run and RBI champion in 1951. Joe Marty's last year with the Solons was 1952. Also in 1952, the PCL's status was upgraded from AAA to "Open Classification." That elevated it over other AAA leagues and gave the PCL a better position when drafting players. In 1953, Bob Dillinger led the PCL in batting by hitting .366.

Tommy Heath managed the Solons in 1956 and 1957, and in spite of being well liked by management, players and fans, he could not produce enough wins to continue in the job. Many consider 1957 to be the last true year of the old PCL and the year that signaled the beginning of the end for the Solons. With the coming of the San Francisco Giants in 1958, Sacramento became part of a smaller market league and game attendance dropped off while financial losses mounted. Also when major league baseball came to the West Coast, the PCL lost its Open Classification status.

1960s

In 1960 baseball games were broadcast on television, and attendance at Solons games plummeted. After a sixth-place finish in the 1960 season, the club was sold and became the Hawaiian Islanders.

1970s

In 1974 the PCL's Eugene Emeralds moved from Oregon to Sacramento and became the Solons. The team established a working agreement with the Milwaukee Brewers and hired Hall-of-Fame pitcher Bob Lemon as manager. The new Solons played at Hughes Stadium on the Sacramento City College campus (near Sutterville Road and Freeport Boulevard). Hughes Stadium had a serious drawback as a ballpark — the 40-foot-high left field fence was reported as being a mere 251 feet from home plate. In fact, measurements determined it was actually only 232 feet away! Sacramentan Bill McNulty hit a record 55 home runs, but it became an "asterisk record" because of the distance and measuring problem.

In the first year, game attendance was very good, but 1975's last-place finish and the "home run derby" atmosphere began to take its toll on the team. In 1975 many of the Solons' better players either moved up or moved on, the quality of play declined, the team finished in last place again, and game attendance dropped. The Milwaukee Brewers felt that Hughes Stadium was not a good place to develop young players, and they ended the agreement with the Solons. In 1976 the Solons did establish a working agreement with the Texas Rangers, but a drastically dropping attendance record forced the team to move to San Jose after the season. Sacramento was without professional baseball until the arrival of the River Cats in 2000.

1974 Players at Hughes Stadium. (Author's Collection).

SACRAMENTO'S PROFESSIONAL BASEBALL TEAMS

1886–1887	Altas
1888	*no team*
1889	Altas
1890–91	Senators
1892	*no team*
1893	Senators
1894–1897	*no team*
1898–1900	Gilt Edge
1901–1903	Senators
1904–1908	*no team*
1909–1914	Senators
1915–1917	*no team*
1918–1935	Senators
1936–1960	Solons
1961–1973	*no team*
1974–1976	Solons
1977–1999	*no team*
2000–present	Sacramento River Cats

1900 Gilt Edge Team featuring Jay Hughes and "Demon" Doyle (Author's Collection).

TEAM NAMES

1880s

The early 1880s semi-pro team, Peruvian Bitters, became the Altas in 1884. A bitter was on old tonic designed to aid in digestion, but usually made with plenty of alcohol and were often served in bars. The Sacramento Altas were named after a famous northern California racehorse who in turn was named for Alta California as California was termed before 1900. The Altas played against the Oakland Greenhood and Morans or G&Ms and the Oakland Colonels.

1890s

The Sacramento Gilt Edge (also called the Brewers) were named after Ruhstaller's top beer. The Gilt Edge played the Santa Cruz Beachcombers, the Stockton Millers, the San Jose Prunepickers and the Oakland Dudes.

1900s

The Sacramento Senators played the San Francisco Wasps. Sacramento players of that time had also played for the Colorado Springs Millionaires, Brooklyn Superbas and Brooklyn Trolley Dodgers (now simply the L.A. Dodgers). In 1906 many former Sacramento players played for the Fresno Raisin Eaters. In 1908 one of Sacramento's opponents was the Santa Cruz Sand Crabs.

1920s & 1920s

Some Sacramento ball players had also played for the Dallas Steers, Bartlesville Blues and Longview Cannibals.

1940s

Some Sacramento ball players had also played for the Chattanooga Lookouts, Johnstown Johnnies and Duluth Dukes.

1950s

Some Sacramento ball players had also played for the Edmonton Eskimos, Little Rock Travelers and New Orleans Pelicans.

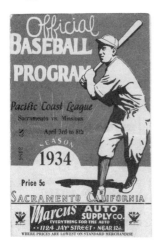

1937

1938-43

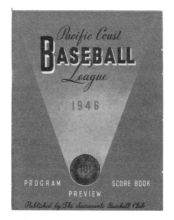

All Author's Collection.

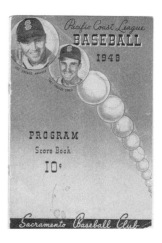

All Author's Collection.

SACRAMENTO BASEBALL PARKS

Sacramento's professional baseball teams played at many home ball parks in the 90 year history covered in this book. "Homefield" for the Altas from 1886-1887 was the infield in the horse race track at Agriculture Park. Agriculture Park was part of the State Fair facilities which were headquartered on the grounds of the State Capitol, but spread around the downtown area.

In 1889 the Altas moved to Snowflake Park which had been built specifically for baseball and modeled after San Francisco's ball park. The park's sponsor was the Hall Luhrs Company whose top whiskey was Snowflake. The whiskey had been named after a legendary race horse. The team was renamed the Senators and they played at Snowflake again in 1890, 1891 and 1893.

The Gilt Edge opened the 1898 season at Snowflake Park, but finished the season at Oak Park which is now called McClatchy Park. The 1889 and 1900 Gilt Edge home games were at Oak Park. The ball park was part of a large complex called Oak Park Recreation Grounds and also Joyland. While the team name changed to the Senators, but the home field remained Oak Park from 1901 through 1902.

1903 marked the beginning of a new era in baseball with the coming of the Pacific Coast League (PCL). The Senators hosted the very first PCL game at Oak Park against the Oakland Oaks on March 26th of that year.

The Senators began play at Buffalo Park in 1910. Buffalo Park was sponsored by the Buffalo Brewing Company which was a major west coast beer supplier from the 1880s through the 1940s. The park was also called Buffalo Recreation Park and one of the early entrances was marked "Recreation Park".

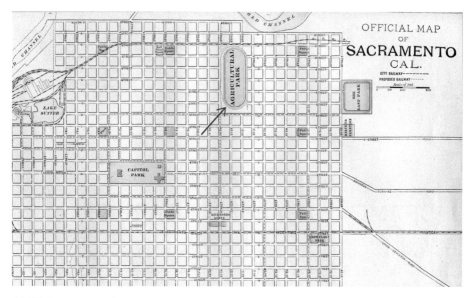

1897 Sacramento City map showing Agricultural Park at the top. (Author Collection).

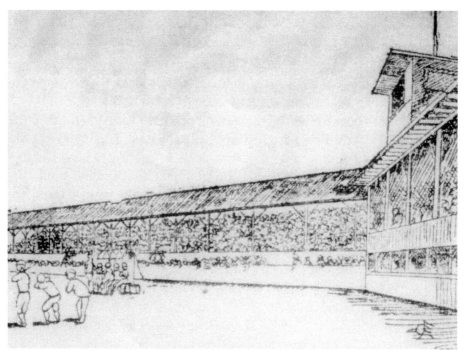

Snowflake Park - "A View Yesterday of the Two Stands" 1890's (Sacramento Archives Museum Collection Center – SAMCC)

Oak Park/Joyland Ball Park in 1900 (Grant Hess Collection)

A player winding up in Buffalo Park in 1913. (Author's Collection)

Moreing Field in 1930, with manager Buddy Ryan's wife Ruby Ryan in front. (Author's Collection) Below: Cardinal Field after the 1938 storm (SAMCC).

Sacramento Boxer Buddy Baer is introduced at a Solons game in 1942 by Ray Mueller in Cardinal Field (Author's Collection). Below: Doubleday Park, 1944 (Author's Collection).

Unseen
In the late 19th century, Sacramento's Agriculture Park was used for bicycle racing and for horse racing during the California State Fair. The infield of the race oval was also used as a baseball field by a number of teams, including the Sacramento Altas in 1886. Unfortunately there are no known photographs of baseball being played there — are there? If you've seen one, we'd love to know about it.

The Moreing brothers bought the Senators in 1920 and tore down Buffalo Park after the 1921 season. The 1922 Senators had a brand new (state of the art for the day) ball park, Moreing Field.

Local banks took over ownership of the Senators for the 1934 and 1935 seasons and while the ball park remained at the corner of Riverside and Broadway, it was referred to as the Sacramento Ball Park.

The St. Louis Cardinals purchased the Sacramento ball club and, from 1936 through 1943, the team was called the Solons and the ball field, Cardinal Field.

When the ball team was sold to a group of local investors in 1944, a fan contest was held and the name changed to Doubleday Park. Dick Edmonds had led the 1944 drive to purchase and retain the team in Sacramento and, after he died, the park was renamed Edmonds Field in 1945.

A night time fire completely destroyed the park in July 1948 forcing the Solons to be "on the road" for the rest of the season. A new Edmonds Field, with a

Sacramento Ball Park

Left: A wooden Edmonds Field. (David Eskinazi Collection). Below: Edmonds Field at Riverside and Broadway; the Tower Theater stands in the foreground. (SAMCC).

Edmonds Field ablaze (Author's Collection).

Edmonds Field rebuilt. (Author's Collection)

concrete grandstand, was ready for the 1949 season. The Solons continued to play at Edmonds until the conclusion of the 1960 season. The ball park was demolished in 1964 and a Target store now occupies the site.

When the Solons returned to Sacramento for the 1974, 1975 and 1976 seasons, Edmonds Field was gone and no other baseball fields were available, so they played their home games at Hughes Stadium, a football field. The short left field fence proved inadequate for "real" baseball and contributed to the Solons leaving again after the 1976 season.

THE HOME FIELD

Park	Location	Team	Years
Agriculture Park	Between 20th & 23rd streets and E and H streets	Altas	1886-87
Snowflake Park	Between 28th & 30th streets and R & S streets	Altas	1889-98
		Senators	1890, 1893
		Gilt Edge	1898
Oak Park/Joyland	*Now McClatchy park*	Gilt Edge	1899-1900
	5th Avenue between	Senators	1900-03
	33rd and 37th Streets	Senators	1909
Buffalo Park	Riverside & Broadway	Senators	1910-1914
			1918-1921
Moreing Field	Riverside & Broadway	Senators	1922-33
Sacramento Baseball Park	Riverside & Broadway	Senators	1934-35
Cardinal Field	Riverside & Broadway	Solons	1936-43
Doubleday Field	Riverside & Broadway	Solons	1944
Edmonds Field	Riverside & Broadway	Solons	1945-60
Hughes Stadium	Sacramento City College	Solons	1974-76

Hughes Stadium (Author's Collection).

RYAN

FITZGERALD

James J. McLaughlin
TRADE MARK

GENUINE
Horace Reich
LOUISVILLE SLUGGER

Solons players' game-used bats (Author's Collection)

GENUINE
Leo Marcoux
LOUISVILLE SLUGGER

BIOGRAPHIES OF SACRAMENTO BALLPLAYERS

Since the late 19th century, Sacramento has been known as a baseball town, and certainly has produced its share of homegrown talent. These Sacramento players are listed chronologically by their first association with a Sacramento baseball team. In this way, the biographies form a timeline of Sacramento's baseball history.

JEROME "ROMEO" BARRY

Jerome D. "Romeo" Barry Sr. was born in Washington Township, Calif., (now part of West Sacramento) in 1859. He was the son of Margaret and Davis B. Barry, who emigrated from Ireland and settled in Washington Township in 1851.

Jerome Barry married Annie Fay in 1886 and their children were Davis B. Barry, Jerome D. Barry Jr., Seth G. Barry, and Ethel Barry McClure.

Barry was well known as an athlete and as a member of the Riverside Rowing Club where he was a champion skiff rower. He pitched professionally for the Sacramento Altas in 1886, and at one

Ray Saracini Collection

time set a state record with 11 consecutive wins. He also pitched for the Altas in 1888 (when they were an "outlaw" semi-professional team and not in the California League) and for the California League San Francisco team in 1889. He later became a respected judge in Washington Township serving from 1913 to 1925. Jerome Barry died in West Sacramento, Calif., in 1931 at age 72.

GEORGE "CHIEF" BORCHERS

George Benard "Chief" Borchers was born in Sacramento on April 18, 1869. His father, George A. Borchers, was one of Sacramento's earliest beer brewers with the City Brewery, and later a saloonkeeper.

Borchers was 5-foot-10 and weighed 180 pounds. A right-handed pitcher, he began playing baseball in 1883 with the amateur Peruvian Bitters club. In 1884, *The Sacramento Bee* called him one of the organizers of the Alta club. He was a talented ballplayer who exhibited erratic behavior and was one of baseball's original "loose cannons." He began his professional career in 1886 when he pitched for Oakland Greenhood and Moran (California League). Later in the season he went back to the Sacramento Altas and continued with them through the 1887 season. On April 23, 1887, *The Sacramento Bee* said, "If Borchers could get command of the ball and his temper, he would soon rank as one of the best pitchers on the coast."

In 1888 Borchers appeared in 10 games for the Chicago White Stockings (National League) with a 4-4 record. While in Chicago, he played with such notables as Cap Anson and Pacific Coast League legend George Van Haltren.

In February 1889, Borchers was arrested for taking a $100 advance from the Stockton ball club and not signing the baseball contract. "He went East," as they said in those days — and was blacklisted from the California League. In July he was arrested for setting fire to his mother's barn after she refused him money. He was observed to be drunk at the time and was also accused of interfering with the fireman at the scene — he claimed he was trying to help. Some research indicates that he played baseball in Detroit in 1889.

In 1890 Borchers was reinstated to the California League and appeared with the Stockton Millers and the Sacramento Altas. On May 12, 1890, *The*

Sacramento Bee reported that he "entered the diamond" for a Sunday game in Stockton drunk and on horseback. During pre-game warm-ups, he was unable to handle the ball and got into a confrontation with his catcher, Mike DePangher.

"Borchers is a great pitcher, but he has no balance wheel, and when he once gets off on a tear, no one can control him," said *The Bee* about his performance that day.

Later in 1890 he played for Portland in the Pacific Northwest League (PNL), but was cut for public drunkenness and moved on to the PNL's Spokane ball team.

In 1891, Borchers pitched for the Oakland Colonels (California League), but little is known about him from 1892 to 1894 except that in 1893 the *Sacramento City Directory* lists him as a baseball player living at 22nd and I streets. In 1895 he had a short-lived stint with the Louisville Colonels of the National League, going 0-1. Little is known of his activities in 1896, but in 1897 he was a player and manager of a semi-professional league team in Kaslo, British Columbia, a mining town.

Final Stop
George Borchers' grave is in the Old City Cemetery, right across the street from the corner of Riverside Boulevard and Broadway, where baseball games were played in Sacramento for more than 50 years. Borchers' final resting place is one of the main stops on the Old City Cemetery's Beer and Baseball walking tour.

In 1898, Borchers appeared with a number of California League teams, including the Santa Cruz Beachcombers and the Stockton Millers. In 1899 he pitched for the San Jose Prunepickers and the Oakland Dudes. He spent 1900 and 1901 with the Dudes.

Borchers and his wife, Ada, had three children: Mary, May and George Jr. When he died in Sacramento on Oct. 24, 1938, George Borchers had operated a dairy in the Natomas area for more than 40 years.

WILLIAM MCLAUGHLIN

William "Tip" McLaughlin was born in Sacramento about 1864. He played organized baseball with various amateur Sacramento baseball clubs until 1884, starting with the Eurekas in 1876.

Sacramento Bee 1887

Missing
Scant information exists about what happened to Billy McLaughlin after 1889. In his book, "History of Baseball in California and Pacific Coast Leagues, 1847-1938," Fred Lange gives us a clue by saying McLaughlin was doing well in Washington State. Can you shed any light on this mystery?

In 1885 he went back East, and played with the Baltimore Orioles and the Washington Nationals. He spent part of the 1886 season with the Savannahs ball club of Savannah, Ga.

In 1886 McLaughlin returned to Sacramento and played for the Sacramento Altas in 1886, 1887 and 1889. He was considered one of the best catchers on the Pacific Coast, in spite of catching "a dozen most erratic twirlers," as *The Sacramento Bee* reported on March 23, 1887. *The Bee's* story also contained high-praise for McLaughlin's overall performance. "As a batter, McLaughlin stands in the front rank, and he has but few equals as a base runner," *The Bee* said. "In fact he is the best all-round baseball player on the Pacific Coast." McLaughlin had many offers to play back East, but decided that the caliber of play and pay would be equal or better by staying with the Altas. His whereabouts after 1889 are unknown.

WILLIAM NEWBERT

Sacramento Bee 1887

William "Billy" Edmond Newbert was born at "Mississippi Bar" in Sacramento County on April 29, 1867. He was the son of pioneers George W. and Mary Jane Millard Newbert. George Newbert had crossed the plains from Maine in 1852 and married Mary Jane in the old Brighton Township (about the only remnant of the township is the old gas station at 7400 Folsom Boulevard in Sacramento). George Newbert had a variety of occupations including miner, railroad worker (for the old Placerville Railroad), and hotel manager (at both the Bruce House and American Eagle Hotels). He was a Sacramento County deputy sheriff for 20 years.

William "Billy" Newbert attended rural Brighton schools, the old Washington Elementary School at 13th and G streets, and Mary J. Watson Grammar School at 16th and J streets (now the site of the Memorial

Auditorium). He began playing baseball in 1883 as a catcher for the local amateur Knickerbockers team.

Newbert played part of the 1886 season with a team called the Snowflakes, and later in the season joined the Sacramento Altas as shortstop. He played for the Altas again in 1887, for Oakland's Greenhood and Moran team (California League) in 1888, and was back with the Altas in 1889. On March 23, 1887, *The Sacramento Bee* described him as "an accurate thrower, a splendid batter and base-runner, and a quiet, gentlemanly representative of the diamond field. ... He plays very gracefully, and is exceedingly popular with the fair devotees of the national game, who never fail to applaud when he makes a good play."

After baseball, Newbert spent some time as a deputy sheriff (finishing his father's unexpired term), and was employed in the retail hardware business both in Sacramento and in Courtland. In 1913 he founded the Newbert Implement Company, which handled farmers' implements and hardware. He retired as company president in 1933, and by the time Newbert's Hardware at 17th and J streets closed in March 1993, it had become one of Sacramento's most respected businesses.

Newbert was a hunter, golfer and a member of the Elks, Masons, and the Native Sons of the Golden West. He never married. He had a sister, Mrs. Jessie Shannon, and four brothers: Frank, George, Monte and Norris Newbert. William Newbert died in Sacramento on Aug. 28, 1944.

Ray Saracini Collection

CHARLES "CHARLEY" ROBERTSON

Charles C. "Charley" Robertson was born in Sacramento on Nov. 6, 1861, and began playing ball as a boy. According to a story in *The Sacramento Bee* on March 30, 1987, he "achieved distinction in 'tom-ball' and 'two-old cat,'" bat and ball games that were similar to baseball. In 1876 he made his start into the baseball arena as a catcher for the amateur Eurekas.

In 1885 Roberston played shortstop for the semi-professional Altas. In 1886 he was again with the Altas when they moved up to the professional level by entering the California League. Robertson moved to second base that year so Billy Newbert could take over as shortstop. He continued at second base in the 1887 season. In its story on March 30, 1987, *The Sacramento Bee* called him "the king of second basemen," and "a cool, calculating player... willing to sacrifice his individual record for the sake of achieving victory for his club — a rare trait in a baseballist."

Mysterious End

Considering that Robertson was such a prominent person, it seems odd that all we know about his death is that he was in an auto accident in the summer of 1921.

The Altas were not included in the California League in 1888, but played at the semi-professional level again. Robertson, who is pictured on the cover of the July 4, 1888, program, was the manager, captain and second baseman that year.

Robertson was employed by Wells Fargo and Company beginning in the 1870s, and in the 1880s served as a "depot agent." In the 1890s, he went to work as an auditor for the city of Sacramento and later became the city tax collector. Years later he co-founded the Robertson-Govan Real Estate Company, and Robertson Way in Sacramento's Land Park is named after him. Charles Robertson died in an automobile accident in 1921.

Author's Collection

ROBERT "RABBIT" McHALE

Robert Emmet "Rabbit" "Bob" McHale was born at Michigan Bluff, Calif., (northeast of Auburn) on Feb. 25, 1872. He was the son of Irish immigrant Patrick McHale. He had a 20-year professional baseball career, much of it in Northern California and particularly in Sacramento.

McHale played for Sacramento in 1889 and 1890 splitting time in the outfield, catching and at third base. In 1891 he appeared in games for three California League teams — San Jose, Oakland and Sacramento. There are no baseball records for McHale in 1892 and 1894, but in 1893 he got into 22 games for the Sacramento Senators (California League), in the outfield, catching, and hitting .359.

In 1895 and 1896 McHale was behind the plate, in the outfield, and at second base for the St. Joseph, Mo. (Western Association) team, hitting a respectable .327 his second year. Later in 1896 McHale played for both Minneapolis and Milwaukee (of the Western League) in every position but pitcher, with a .309 batting average. He spent the 1897 season as a regular outfielder for the Toronto Maple Leafs (Eastern League) where he hit .292.

"Rabbit" McHale began the 1898 season with a short six-game stay with Sacramento's Gilt Edge, hitting .391. During the rest of the 1898 season, McHale bounced from team to team getting into 121 games with the Washington Senators (National League), Rochester-Ottawa (Eastern League), Hamilton (Canadian League) and Sacramento (Pacific Coast League). Although it has the same name, this Pacific Coast League is not the same long-standing PCL formed in 1903.

In 1899 McHale spent some time with the Gilt Edge, but was in the outfield most of the season in the East with Rochester/Hartford (Eastern League) and Bristol (Connecticut League). In 1900 he went west again, splitting time with Pueblo (Western League) and the Stockton Millers (California League). McHale packed his bags again in 1901, playing for the San Francisco Wasps (California League), the Colorado Springs Millionaires (Western League) and the Denver Grizzlies (Western League). In 1902 he settled down to become a regular outfielder (119 games) for the San Francisco Wasps.

From 1903 through 1907 McHale found some stability as a regular outfielder for the Denver Grizzlies where he hit .270.

McHale returned to Sacramento later in 1907, playing for the Senators (then in the outlaw California League), in both 1907 and 1908. He finished his professional career with the Senators in 1909 when they again became part of the PCL. After his baseball career, McHale worked for 35 years as a carpenter for Pacific Gas and Electric Company. He died in Sacramento on June 9, 1952.

JAMES "JAY" HUGHES

James "Jay" Hughes was born in Sacramento on Jan. 22, 1874. He played in local leagues in Sacramento in the early 1890s, and began pitching

professionally for the Victoria, British Columbia, team (North West League) in 1896. He was "discovered" on Nov. 26, 1897, when he was pitching for Sacramento's semi-professional Gilt Edge against the touring Baltimore Orioles (National League). In front of 5,000 avid baseball fans, he shut out 12 batters, while allowing only three hits. Orioles' manager Ned Hanlon brought Hughes back East to pitch for the Baltimore Orioles in 1898 and the Brooklyn Superbas (National League) in 1899. In Brooklyn, he had a league-leading 28-6 mark. (Hughes' older brother, Michael J. "Mickey" Hughes, had played professionally from 1888 through 1890, winning 25 games for the 1888 Brooklyn Trolley-Dodgers.) Jay Hughes was married in 1900, and at the request of his new wife decided to stay in Sacramento and play for the Gilt Edge, where he went 23-9.

This decision was made easier when local businesses matched the salary Brooklyn had offered him. He pitched again for the Brooklyn Superbas (National League) in 1901 and 1902, accumulating a lifetime major league record of 83 and 41 with a 3.00 ERA. Hughes preferred the West Coast, so he returned to pitch for four years in the Pacific Coast League. From 1903 through 1904 he was with the Seattle Indians and from 1906 through 1907 with the San Francisco Seals winning 61 games and losing 34 with a 2.50 ERA during those four years. A back injury in 1907 ended his career.

No Idea

When I attended elementary school in the mid-1950s, school children walked and played upon the train trestle that Jay Hughes fell from. We had no idea that the baseball player had fallen to his death there three decades before.

In 1908 Hughes became a "driver" (presumably of wagons), and from 1909 through 1911 he held various jobs with the city streets department. In 1912 and 1913, he worked as a gardener at the state Capitol. Later on, he was a bartender and then a groundskeeper at the Sutterville baseball diamond. He had four children: Jay Junior, who played baseball for Cleveland in 1923, Edward, Margaret and Marjorie. In the 1930s, many local baseball fans thought Hughes was the greatest pitcher of all time and the man who perfected the "famous fade away ball," for which New York Giants' legend Christy

Mathewson later became famous. "Jay" Hughes died in Sacramento on June 2, 1924, from head injuries sustained when he fell from a train trestle near Sutterville Road (near where the Sacramento Zoo is today).

CHARLES "DEMON" DOYLE

Charles Francis "Charley" "Demon" Doyle was born in San Jose, Calif., on Nov. 13, 1875. The 5-foot-11 Doyle was raised in San Jose, the son of parents who came around Cape Horn from Ireland in the 1860s.

Doyle had a long baseball career that included nine years of professional play and several more years with semi-professional teams. He began his professional career as a pitcher for the 1896 Oakland team (California League). He appeared with the independent Oakland Reliance team in 1897. He is, perhaps, best remembered as the dominant pitcher on the "three-peat" California League Champion Sacramento Gilt Edge of 1898, 1899 and 1900. In those years, he posted 10-5, 28-11 and 19-18 records, respectively. He also played in 1901 and 1902 for Sacramento's California League team when it was renamed the Senators. In 1901 he went 20-12, but hurt his arm later in the season. Because he could no longer be a regular pitcher, he moved to the outfield in 1902.

In 1903 "Demon" continued with the Sacramento Senators when they became part of the newly formed Pacific Coast League. He played various positions, primarily in the outfield.

When the Sacramento team was sold to Tacoma, Wash., and became the Tacoma Tigers, Doyle went with them, playing second base and in the outfield when they won the 1904 PCL championship. He played for the Tigers again in 1905, but the team finished in last place. His teammates with the Tigers were "Truck" Eagan, Jack Fitzgerald, Charlie Graham, Bobby Keefe and Tommy Sheehan.

In 1906 he was a player-manager for the Fresno Raisin Eaters (PCL), and in addition to pitching, he played second base, shortstop and in the outfield.

From 1907 through 1908, "Demon" Doyle was an infielder for the Sacramento Senators (in the outlaw California State League). One of his

Flames

I had a cup of coffee with newspaperman Stan Gilliam in 2006, who told me about "Demon" Doyle's cigar shop at 730 K St. Gilliam's father had taken Stan there because he wanted him to see where the city's "sports-minded men" gathered, and to meet the "Demon" himself. A 5-year-old at the time, Stan mostly remembers being fascinated by the blue gas flame that was always on so gentlemen could light their cigars.

teammates was future Red Sox Hall-of-Fame outfielder Harry Hooper.

In 1909 Doyle was again with the Senators as they returned to the PCL. In 1910 and again in 1912, he appeared with the Sacramento Junior Lawmakers (California State League). In 1910, he also managed the team.

Doyle retired after the 1912 season and opened a cigar store at 730 K St. in Sacramento. For many years the store was a gathering place for "sportsmen" of the area. Some "tokens" the store issued have survived and list the Senators' 1914 game schedule on the back.

Dominant Demon
Doyle earned his "Demon" nickname because of his dominance on the pitching mound in the early part of his career.

The Sacramento Archives and Museum Collection Center has a portrait of Doyle (dated 1914) in a baseball uniform with "San Diego" on the front, but the team and league are unknown.

In 1920 Lew Moreing hired "Demon" Doyle to be secretary of the Sacramento Senators. He held that position until 1936.

Doyle and his wife, Alma, raised their children, Charles, Chester, Jackson, Stanley and Vivian, in the family home at 30th and I streets in Sacramento. On Sept. 1, 1949, after Doyle had been honored with an "old-timers day," Sacramento Bee writer Vince Stanich lauded the player, saying, "Demon Doyle has been identified with baseball in Sacramento since 1898." Charles Doyle died in Sacramento on Dec. 9, 1950.

TOMMY SHEENAN

SAMCC

Thomas H. Sheehan was born in Sacramento on Nov. 6, 1877. He began playing baseball in local amateur leagues, eventually moving up to the professional level.

The 5-foot-8, 160-pound right-hander was on the famed Sacramento Gilt Edge teams that won three California League championships in a row from 1898 through 1900. In 1898 Sheehan was an outfielder. In 1899 he was an infielder, and in 1900, he was back in the outfield. He also got into one game with the New York Giants in 1900.

Demon Doyle, (Author's Collection)

Author's Collection

In 1901 Sheehan returned to Sacramento and moved back to the infield where he remained for the rest of his career, primarily as a third baseman. When the Senators moved to the PCL in 1903, Sheehan played a prominent role. He appeared in 193 games at third base with a .263 batting average. He hit .292 with the team when they became the PCL champion Tacoma Tigers in 1904. He also was a regular with the Tigers in 1905.

Sheehan played for the Pittsburgh Pirates (National League) in 1906 at third base in 95 games alongside Honus Wagner at shortstop, hitting .289. He was with the Pirates again in 1907, hitting .310 in 75 games. In 1908 he became a regular with the Brooklyn Superbas (National League) hitting .261 in 146 games. His lifetime MLB batting average was .280.

In 1909 Sheehan played third base for Oakland (California League). In 1910 he was back in the PCL at third base, this time with the Portland Beavers, where he played in 110 games. He appeared in 184 games for the Beavers in 1911.

Sheehan finished his career playing in 105 games at third base for the 1912 Sacramento Senators where he hit .261. He had the good fortune to play on four championship teams! He died in Panama City, Panama, on May 22, 1959.

JOHN "FIREMAN" FITZGERALD

John Patrick "Fireman" Fitzgerald was born in California on March 8, 1881. The 5-foot-10 right-hander pitched in the Pacific Coast League for eight years.

Fitzgerald began his PCL career with the 1903 Sacramento Senators, pitching in 45 games with a 14-24 record. Lacking adequate gate receipts, in 1904 the Sacramento ball club moved to Tacoma, Wash., becoming the Tacoma Tigers. Fitzgerald had a good year — posting a 17-12 record and a 3.26 ERA — and helped the Tigers win the 1904 PCL championship.

In 1905 Fitzgerald went 16-24 for the Tigers, and in 1906 he went 24-26 for the Fresno Raisin Eaters. There are no known baseball records for Fitzgerald for 1907 and 1908.

In 1909, Fitzgerald was back with the Senators. From 1909 through 1912, he pitched in 163 games with a combined record of 53-82. He did not have the best control, as he averaged 20-plus hit batters per season! Fitzgerald's ERA was 2.50 in 1909; 2.51 in 1910; and 2.37 in 1911. He closed out his PCL career with Sacramento in 1912. Fitzgerald is perhaps best remembered for one Sunday in 1911 when he pitched against Portland, Ore. The game went

24 innings. He allowed only 10 hits and one run, and the game ended in a 1-1 tie because of darkness.

After baseball, Fitzgerald earned his living as hotel clerk, including 18 years at the Lenhart Hotel, 1121 Ninth St., in Sacramento. His wife's name was Virginia, and he had a brother, Daniel, and two sisters, Katherine and Frances.

In a story in *The Sacramento Bee* on Dec. 3, 1947, Fitzgerald commented on the stamina of pitchers of the day, saying, "Modern day hurlers are too fragile," and adding that he used to work "every other day and never heard of a sore arm." John Fitzgerald died in Sacramento on Dec. 2, 1947.

Robert Keefe Collection

ROBERT "BOBBY" KEEFE

Robert "Bobby" Francis Keefe was born in Folsom, Calif., on June 16, 1882. Keefe's father came from upstate New York, and traveled around Cape Horn to California during the Gold Rush, ending up in Folsom as a successful open-pit gold miner. Because of the family's financial success, Keefe went to boarding school (for high school and college) at what is now the University of Santa Clara, where he excelled on the baseball teams and was a teammate of Charlie Graham.

The 5-foot-11, 155-pound right-hander was a pitcher in the Pacific Coast League for five years, beginning with the Sacramento Senators in 1903, where he was 15-14 with a 2.96 ERA. When the Senators moved to Tacoma, Wash., and became the Tigers in 1904, Keefe went with them, going 34-16 with a 2.40 ERA for the 1904 PCL champs. He also led the league in shutouts that year. In 1905 he led with a 30-19 record and a 1.61 ERA for the Tigers.

In 1906 Keefe went 7-6 for the Montreal Royals (Eastern League). In 1907 he moved up to pitch for the New York Highlanders, where he was 3-5 with a respectable 2.79 ERA. Later in 1907, he returned to Montreal, where he was a regular on the mound through the 1910 season, posting a 54-55 record over the four years.

Keefe pitched for the Cincinnati Reds from 1911 to 1912, going 13-16 over the two-year period. Near the end of the 1912 season, he joined the Rochester Hustlers (International League), where he pitched through the 1914 season with a 45-25 three-year record.

In 1915 Keefe got into 13 games with the Portland Beavers (Pacific Coast League). From 1916 through 1920, he was out of organized professional baseball, but returned in 1921 to appear in 10 games for the San Francisco Seals (PCL). His last year as a player was 1921.

Keefe has the distinction of pitching the only PCL no-hitter at a neutral site, when Tacoma beat Oakland at San Jose in 1904. Because of the game's location, many of Keefe's friends and former teammates from Santa Clara were there. Attendance in Tacoma, however, was so poor that year that the Tigers played most of their games on the road.

Keefe married in Cincinnati, Ohio, in 1912, and he and his wife, Margaret, had four children: Helen, Carol, Robert and John. After baseball, Keefe lived in Folsom where he was a successful rancher and worked as a county assessor and postmaster. He died in Sacramento on Dec. 6, 1964.

ROSS "BRICK" ELDRED

Ross C. "Brick" Eldred was born in Sacramento on July 26, 1892. He excelled in baseball at Sacramento High School and graduated in 1910. After demonstrating his skills in local leagues, the 5-foot-6, 175-pounder turned professional at age 20, playing in the outfield in the Pacific Coast League for 13 seasons, with Salt Lake City, Seattle, and Sacramento.

"Brick" appeared in 1,709 games, had 2,034 hits, 516 doubles (25 percent of his hits were doubles), stole 219 bases and finished with a lifetime batting average of .332. He began his career in 1916 with the Salt Lake City Bees and played with the Newark Bears (International League) in 1917. He joined the Sacramento Senators in 1918,

ZEE-NUT
SERIES
1919
ELDRED
SACTO.

Author's Collection

Mails.
Clev.

Frederick
Foto

and remained with the team into 1920. Later in the 1920 season, he moved to the Seattle Indians, playing with them through 1928, including the 1924 PCL championship season.

In 1929 Eldred played for the Wichita Falls (Texas) Spudders (Texas League), and finished his career back with the Senators in 1930, hitting .369. Known for his batting average, base stealing and doubles hitting, Eldred was elected to the Pacific Coast League Hall of Fame in 2003.

Eldred married in 1914. He and his wife, Myrtle, had a son, Richard. Eldred retired after working for many years at the California Almond Growers Exchange. He was an avid golfer, playing for nearly 70 years and shooting a 79 when he was 79. He was elected to the La Salle Hall of Fame and the Marysville Old-timers Hall of Fame. He died in Sacramento on Dec. 22,1976.

JOHN "DUSTER" MAILS

John Walter "The Great," "The Imperial Duster," "Duster" Mails was born on Oct. 1, 1894, in San Quentin, Calif., where his mother was postmistress. When his father was hired by the Southern Pacific Railroad, the family moved to Sacramento. Mails played baseball for Christian Brothers High School when it was at 12th and K streets. He also played in the Sacramento Winter League and later played baseball and basketball at St. Mary's College in Moraga, Calif.

Mails was a pitcher in the Pacific Coast League for 14 years, starting in 1917 with the Portland Beavers, and playing for Sacramento from 1919 through 1920. In his PCL career, "Duster" won 173 and lost 171 with a 3.90 ERA. His left-handed fastball earned him "The Imperial Duster" nickname. Mails was in the U.S. military during World War I.

He also played seven years in the majors: for the Brooklyn Robins (National League) from 1915 to 1916; the Cleveland Indians (American League) from 1920 to 1922; and for the St. Louis Cardinals (National League) from 1925 to 1926. His major league record was 32 and 25 with a 4.10 ERA. At the height of his career in 1920, he struck out Eddie Collins, Buck Weaver and Joe Jackson with the bases loaded. He pitched 15 2/3 scoreless innings in a 1-0 victory in a 1920 World Series game. The Cleveland Indians won that World Series, five games to two, over the Brooklyn Dodgers. A shoulder injury cut Mails' baseball career short, but he worked for many years in public relations for both the San Francisco Seals and Giants. He retired in 1972, and became a member of the Sacramento Athletic Hall of Fame. John Mails died in San Francisco on July 5, 1974.

EARL "PINCHES" KUNZ

Earl Dewey "Pinches" "Pinch" Kunz was born in Sacramento on Dec. 25, 1899. He started in baseball on the local sandlots, broke into professional baseball with the Sacramento Senators, and went up to the majors with the Pittsburgh Pirates. His nickname "Pinches" and "Pinch" evolved from an earlier nickname "Pinchers," referring to the attacking methods of a crab. He and "Kettle" Wirts formed the "battery" of a sandlot team in the 12th and U streets neighborhood for the old Patterson Hatters (Sacramento Winter League), for the Southside Park team, and later for Plymouth (Amador Mine League).

Author's Collection

ZEE-NUT
SERIES
1920
KUNZ
SACTO.

Kunz's pitching in the semi-pro leagues caught the attention of Sacramento player Ray Keating, who recommended that Lew Moreing sign Kunz to a Senators' contract. He pitched for the Senators from 1920 through 1922. "Pinch had a hard fast one and the right-hander was a pretty good hitter, too, for a pitcher," said "Kettle" Wirts in a story in *The Sacramento Bee* on April 15, 1963. Kunz's PCL career batting average was .272.

Kunz pitched for the Pittsburgh Pirates in 1923, with a 2-5 record and a 4.00 ERA. He played for the Oakland Oaks (PCL) from 1924 to 1926 and for the San Francisco Seals (PCL) from 1926 to 1927 and went 61 and 66 during those four years.

On April 15, 1963, *The Bee* also reported some of the comments Ray Keating made about Kunz, his Sacramento Senators teammate in 1928. "(Kunz) helped us in that stretch drive as we beat San Francisco for the second-half flag," Keating said. "Pinch had a lot of stuff on the ball and he was great guy, too. He was real witty and he gave us a lot of laughs."

In 1929 Kunz appeared in 14 games for the Senators and the Seattle Indians (PCL) with a 4-5 record. He finished his professional baseball career with the Indians in 1930, appearing in 44 games with an 8-8 record. His PCL record as a pitcher for 10 seasons was 109-128 with a 4.37 ERA.

Later in life Kunz took an avid interest in owning and training racehorses, and spent a lot of time in the "Fair Circuit." He died in Sacramento on April 14, 1963.

KENNETH PENNER

Kenneth William Penner was born on April 24, 1896, in Boonville, Ind. The 6-foot, 170-pounder threw with his right hand and batted with his left. He began his professional baseball career as a pitcher for the Columbus, Miss., Joy Riders (Cotton States League) in 1913 at the age of 17, and stayed in the game in various capacities for more than 40 years.

In 1914, Penner played in 38 games for the Cadillac Chiefs (Michigan State League) with a 14-18 record. He appeared in two games for the Grand Rapids Champs, and in 37 games with an 18-14 record for the Keokuk Indians (Central Association) during the 1915 season.

In 1916 Penner had a short, four-game stay with the Cleveland Indians (American League), where he was 1-0. Also that season he got into 35 games for the Marshalltown Ansons (Central Association) and posted a 22-11 record and a league leading ERA of 1.41.

In 1917, Penner pitched for the Portland Beavers with a 21-18 record and 3.33 ERA. When the Beavers were disbanded before the 1918 season, Penner ended up with the Salt Lake City Bees where he had a 7-5 record. When a new Beavers team was formed for the 1919 season, he was back with them, and he posted a 15-20 record.

After the 1919 season, Penner was traded to Sacramento. He remained with the Senators from 1920 through 1923. He was part of the regular pitching rotation and compiled a 59-71 record over those four years. Penner's lifetime PCL batting average was a respectable (for a pitcher) .241, and he hit .319 for Sacramento in 1921.

Penner pitched for the Vernon Tigers (PCL) from 1924 through 1925 with a combined 26-19 record. In 1925 he also went 19-6 in 29 games for the

Wichita (Kan.) Izzies (Western League).

From 1926 through 1928, Penner pitched for the Houston Buffalos (Texas League), appearing in 114 games with a 50-34 record over the three years. He led the league in ERAs in 1927 with 2.54.

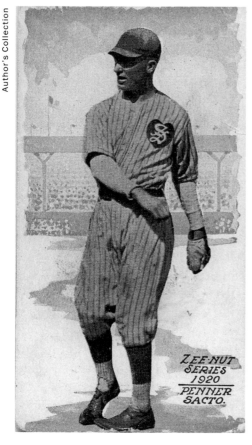

In 1929 Penner pitched in five games for the Chicago Cubs with an 0-1 record and in 24 games with a 13-7 record for the Indianapolis Indians (American Association).

From 1930 through 1935, Penner pitched in 179 games for the Louisville (Ky.) Colonels (American Association) with a combined 55-50 record over the six-year period. He also managed the Colonels during the 1934 and 1935 seasons.

In 1936 Penner managed the Crookston (Minn.) Pirates (Northern League), putting himself in to pitch in 23 games with a 6-4 record. He managed the 1937 Montgomery (Ala.) Bombers (Southeastern League), again pitching, but this time in only three games with no decisions.

Penner managed the 1938 and 1939 Bellingham Chinooks (Western International League). He pitched in four games in 1938 with an 0-3 record. In 1940, he managed the Pocatello Cardinals (Pioneer League), part of the St. Louis farm system.

In 1941 Penner coached for the Solons with one player appearance as pitcher. In 1942 he not only coached, but also pitched in 12 games and was part of that PCL Championship season. He managed the Solons in 1943, but unfortunately the parent club dispersed the players from the 1942 season because of World War II. Without adequate talent, the Solons had a 41-114 year, the worst in PCL history, and the Cardinals ended their relationship with Sacramento.

Penner's last year as a manager was in 1944, when he skippered the Rochester Redwings, the Cardinals AA farm club (International League). After the 1944 season, he scouted for the St. Louis Cardinals. He discovered many fine young ballplayers including Clem Driesewerd, Tommy Glaviano, Gordon Jones and "Nippy" Jones. Kenneth Penner died in Sacramento on May 28, 1959.

JOHN "BUDDY" RYAN

John Budd "Buddy" Ryan was born on a ranch near Plainville, Kan., on Oct. 6, 1885, and moved to Denver when he was 2. His father had emigrated from Ireland and was a Denver police officer for 30 years.

Ryan began playing professional baseball as an outfielder with the Grand Island ball club (Nebraska League) in 1906. In 1907 he moved up to the Pueblo Indians ball club (Western League).

In 1908, Ryan moved to the Portland Beavers (Pacific Coast League), where he played for manager Walter McCredie. He played with the Beavers for four years through the 1911 season and developed into a fine batsman, posting a .333 average in 1911.

"Buddy" played for the Cleveland Indians (American League) from 1912 through 1913, posting a .282 batting average. He went back to the Portland Beavers for the 1914 season. In 1915 he was traded to the Salt Lake City Bees (PCL) where he spent the next four seasons in the outfield, hitting .321. Ryan played in the outfield for the Sacramento Senators from 1920 to 1925 and ended his PCL playing career in Sacramento with a .295 lifetime batting average.

He replaced Charlie Pick as the Senators manager in 1924, and managed the team until 1932,

Author's Collection

Buddy Ryan (Author's Collection)

longer than any other Sacramento manager. He proved to be a capable manager and, in spite of limited team talent, produced a 735-792 record (.481). He also guided the Senators through the second-half championship in the 1928 season. Ryan was adept at developing local sandlot talent, which proved profitable to team owner Lew Moreing who, in turn, sold those players to National and American league teams. Some of them were Frank DeMaree, Hank Steinbacker, Stan Hack, Myril Hoag, Alex Kampouris, Earl McNeely and Merv Shea.

In 1935 Ryan took over as manager of the Portland Beavers, posted a 21-33 record, and was replaced in June. In 1944 "Dolph" Camilli, one of Ryan's protégés, hired him as a coach for the Oakland Oaks (PCL). In 1946 "Buddy" managed the Wenatchee (Wash.) Chiefs of the eight-team Western International League to the pennant. For his efforts he was named "Wenatchee Sports Personality of the Year."

Ryan was well liked in and out of baseball circles, and after he retired from baseball he returned to Sacramento. He and his wife, Ruby, operated a service station near the ballpark for many years, and later owned a restaurant. Ryan was also an avid duck hunter and managed the Sacramento Gun Club for years. He was elected to the Pacific Coast League Hall of Fame in 2004. He died in Sacramento on July 9, 1956.

Lumber of Legend

"Buddy" Ryan was one of the first "sluggers" of baseball, and consequently, one of the few early ball players who had his own bat — the "Buddy" Ryan model bat was one of the most popular models of the day. I am proud to say that among my most prized early Sacramento baseball artifacts is a "Buddy" Ryan bat (and, of course, a couple of bats that Buddy used during games).

EARL MCNEELY

Earl George McNeely was born in Sacramento on May 12, 1898, and began his athletic career as a soccer and basketball player on Sacramento city's fields and courts. He was a member of the Sacramento American Legion team that won the basketball championship of the Amateur Athletic Union in 1922. McNeely did not begin playing organized baseball until after he returned from service in World War I and played for the Leo Lobner team of the National Division of the Sacramento Winter League.

Sacramento Senators' owner Lew Moreing was adept at finding and developing local talent, and McNeely was one of his best finds. The 5-foot-9, 155-pounder played second base, third base, and in the outfield for the Senators from 1922 to 1924. He usually played center field and was regarded as one of the fastest men in the Pacific Coast League. His stellar play brought about his sale to the Washington (D.C.) Senators (American League) for the then hefty price of $35,000, and three players.

After some initial questions about his physical condition and a slow start, McNeely turned out to be a solid contributor to Washington's 1924 World Series championship. The Senators, the long-time doormats of the American League, captured their first World Series when McNeely's bouncer hit a pebble and hopped high over Freddy Lindstrom's head, producing a 4-3 win. The play has been described as one of the most exciting moments in World Series history. It gave Hall-of-Fame manager "Bucky" Harris and the Washington Senators their only World Series championship and Hall-of-Fame pitcher Walter "The Big Train" Johnson his only World Series victory.

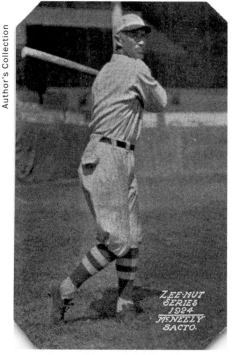

From 1924 through 1927, McNeely continued to play for Washington, primarily in the outfield, but sometimes at first base. In 1925 and 1926, he was a solid contributor to the team, playing in 122 games batting .286, and in 124 games batting .303, respectively. He also appeared in the 1925 World Series, but the Senators lost to the Pittsburgh Pirates three games to four. In 1927, at the age of 29, McNeely's skills began to diminish and his batting average began to dip.

He was sent to the Saint Louis Browns (American League) for the 1928 season, where he appeared in 127 games. As his batting average went down, he appeared in fewer games for the Browns, and he was released after the 1931 season. His major league lifetime batting average was .272.

In 1932 he was back with the Sacramento Senators and got into 100 games. That same year, he replaced "Buddy" Ryan as team manager, and continued through 1934 with a winning percentage of .534. In 1933, he played in 94 games, hitting .308. His last year as a player was 1934, when he appeared in just 26 games, hitting .289. He ended his career with a Sacramento lifetime batting average of .294.

In 1934, when Lew Moreing was unable to make his loan payments on the team, a group of local banks took over the ownership of the Senators, naming McNeely as team president. In 1935 he turned the managerial duties over to "Kettle" Wirts. Poor team performance led to Wirts' dismissal in June, and McNeely again became manager as well as president. Continued poor performance led to the purchase of the team by the St. Louis Cardinals and McNeely's dismissal from the club after the 1935 season.

In 1936 and 1937, he returned to Washington to coach for the Senators. Later he came back to Orangevale, where he worked at real estate, investments, and in the farming and cattle business, He retired in 1959.

McNeely was very community minded. Beginning in 1933, he served for a couple of years as a member of the Orangevale Volunteer Fire Department. He later became director of the Citrus Heights Fire District and was the first president of the Sacramento County Fire Directors Association. He was a trustee for Orangevale Elementary Schools and American River College. He was active with the Granite Soil Conservation District and president of the Sacramento County Fair board of directors. He even ventured into politics as an unsuccessful candidate for county supervisor.

McNeely and his wife, Ethel, had a daughter, Carol. He was active in the Masons and was an avid golfer. He was inducted into the Sacramento Athletic Hall of Fame and the La Salle Hall of Fame, and died in Sacramento on July 16, 1971.

CLAUDE ROHWER

Claude Rohwer was born in Dixon, Calif., on May 11, 1897. The 5-foot-11, 165-pound right-hander had a four-year professional baseball career as a middle infielder (second base, third base and shortstop).

Rohwer began his career in 1920 by getting into two games as shortstop for the San Francisco Seals (Pacific Coast League). He was out of baseball

Author's Collection

in 1921, but came back with the Charleston Pals in the South Atlantic League ("Sally League") hitting .294 in 116 games.

Rohwer became a regular with his home area Sacramento Senators in 1923, playing all the middle infield positions and hitting .295. His last professional baseball season was in 1924 when he hit .284 for the Senators in 120 games at third base.

Claude's brother Ray played for the Senators from 1926 through 1931. Rohwer served in the U.S. Army during World War I and later became a prominent attorney in Northern California. He died in Woodland, Calif., on Oct. 7, 1940. On Oct. 9, 1940, *The Woodland Daily Democrat* reported that Rohwer's funeral was "one of the largest ever held in Solano County" and "Dixon business houses closed during the funeral hour so that clerks and owners alike might attend the services."

LEONARD "LENNIE" BACKER

Leonard Henry "Lennie" Backer was born on Feb. 5, 1907, in Franklin, Calif., and raised on the family dairy farm. Nicknamed the "Franklin Milkman," the 5-foot-9, 165-pound right-hander played baseball for four years at Sacramento High School, graduating in 1925. He also played for the Franklin team in the Sacramento County League. "Lennie" was signed by the Sacramento Senators right out of high school and played in the infield, primarily third base, from 1925 to 1933. When his father told him that he had to work as a dairy farmer rather than a ballplayer, Backer negotiated a compromise by buying his father a milking machine. He appeared in 14 games in 1925, spending much of his time learning from the veteran players.

In 1926 the "Milkman" had an outstanding spring training playing second base for the "Yannigans" — Senators players who scrimmaged against the "regulars." Backer played so well that he put Senators' management into a dilemma. According to a photocopy of a clipping from an unidentifiable newspaper found in a scrapbook, Backer had a great arm, and "was a proven batsman and a fielder who stops everything that comes his way ... too good to be kept on a bench." However, in spite of his obvious talent, Backer was unable to break into a high-caliber infield that included Earl Sheely at first base, Johnny Monroe at second base, Ray French at shortstop, and Jimmy McLaughlin at third base. Backer was "farmed" to the Twin Falls Bruins (Utah-Idaho League), where he led the league in batting with a .374 average.

In 1927 Backer was back with the Senators as a reserve infielder. He appeared in 27 games that year for the aging Johnny Monroe, who some considered to be the best second-baseman in the PCL. In 1928 Backer got his chance, took over at third base, and was an integral part of the famous 1928 team that won the PCL second-half championship.

From 1929 through 1930, Backer performed at a high level, both with his glove and his bat. His batting average was .334 in 1929 and .330 in 1930.

In the early 1930s, Backer was a rising star with the Senators and was attracting major league scouts from many teams. However, his career and his life almost ended on April 27, 1931, when he was hit on the head by a pitched ball in a game against the San Francisco Seals at the newly opened Seals Stadium. A fastball served up by "Wild Bill" Henderson hit Backer on the side of the head and fractured his skull. His teammates said that he did not move his head at all — Backer later explained that he had lost the ball in the big white letters of a sign in center field. He was unconscious for 48 hours and in the hospital for six weeks. The 1931 baseball season was over for the "Milkman," and he required surgery again in 1942 for the same injury.

Author's Collection

While that incident put Backer's baseball career on hold, it launched a future major-league star. Stan Hack took over at third base for the remainder of the 1931 season and was sold to Chicago Cubs (National League) at the end of the season.

Backer recovered from the beaning in time for the 1932 season and again became a steady performer for the Senators. He batted .313 in 1932 and .333 in 1933. Because of the injury, however, scouts were wary, and Backer never moved up to the major leagues.

In 1934 Backer was sold to the San Francisco Seals where he became teammates with Joe Marty and Joe DiMaggio. The 1935 Seals won the pennant, and after the season, Backer went on a 12-game barnstorming tour with some of the other players, including Joe Marty. The tour started in Fresno and ended in Eureka. While the expectation was to make some money, Backer returned home with the same amount of money he had in his pocket when he left. His lifetime Pacific Coast League career batting average was .313, and he felt that he had played for two of the greatest PCL managers — "Buddy" Ryan and Lefty O'Doul of the Seals.

Backer spent most of the 1936 season with the Syracuse Chiefs (International League), and part of the 1937 season with the Houston Buffalos (Texas League). He became a player-manager for the (Waterloo) Red Hawks, a farm club for the Cincinnati Reds, in the "Three-Eye" League, also called the "Three I" League because it included Illinois, Indiana and Iowa. The Hawks finished second in 1937 and 1938.

Backer retired from baseball after the 1938 season, returned to dairy farming in Franklin, and later bought his own farm. He retired in 1967.

Backer married Edlo Kripp, niece of Edward Kripp. (Kripp had an interest in Buffalo Park from 1910 until World War I and had managed the Sacramento Gilt Edge in the late 1890s.) The Backers had two daughters, Barbara and Janet. "Lennie" belonged to several agricultural organizations and was a life member of the National Rifle Association. He was elected to the La Salle Hall of Fame in 1972, and died in Sacramento on Oct. 20, 1989.

MYRIL HOAG

Myril Oliver Hoag was born in Davis, Calif., on March 9, 1908. His maternal grandparents had crossed the plains from Missouri and settled in Davisville (now Davis) in the 1840s. His father, Tracy Hoag, pitched for the 1908 Stockton Millers, the 1908 Santa Cruz Sand Crabs, the 1909 Fresno

Raisin Growers and the 1910 Fresno Tigers in the old California League.

Hoag was 5-foot-11 and weighed 180 pounds. An outfielder, he threw and batted right-handed, and enjoyed a 24-year professional baseball career, including 13 seasons in the majors. He played ball in the semi-professional Sacramento Valley League, spending parts of the 1926 season with the Woodland and Maxwell teams.

Hoag's talent got him onto the Sacramento Senators roster at the end of the 1926 season. In 1927 he was farmed out to the Twin Falls Bruins (Utah-Idaho League), but also got into four games for Sacramento. He was out of organized baseball during the 1928 season.

From 1929 through 1930, Hoag was a regular in the outfield for the Sacramento Senators. After an outstanding season in 1930 — when he hit .337 in 188 games — Lew Moreing sold Hoag to the New York Yankees.

Author's Collection

Hoag played in the outfield for the Yankees from 1931 to 1938, and was on three World Series championship teams: 1932, 1937 and 1938, when the Yankees beat Joe Marty's Cubs.

From 1939 to 1941, Hoag played for the St. Louis Browns, and was an American League All-Star in 1939. Late in the 1941 season, Hoag was traded to the Chicago White Sox where he played through the 1942 season. He was out of organized baseball in 1943 while serving in the Air Force during World War II. In 1944 he was back with the ChiSox but was traded to the Cleveland Indians later that season. He got into 40 games for the Indians in 1945, his last MLB season. His lifetime MLB batting average was .271.

In 1946 Hoag became a player-manager for the Palatka Azaleas (Florida State League), playing in 121 games with a league-leading .342 batting average. In 1947 he was again a player-manager in the Florida State League,

this time for the Gainesville G-Men, where he played 102 games and again led the league in batting with a .350 average.

Hoag managed and played for Gainesville again in 1948 and in 1949, hitting .326 in 59 games and .317 in 62 games, respectively. He also spent part of the 1949 season with the St. Petersburg Saints (Florida International League), appearing in four games. In 1950 Hoag was the player-manager for the Rome Red Sox (Georgia-Alabama League). His final professional season was 1951, when he managed and played for Gainesville.

It is interesting to note that while Hoag was an outfielder for the first 18 years of his career (although he did have three MLB pitching appearances), he pitched in 182 games between 1946 and 1951, posting a 91-46 record. After his baseball career, he worked in the trucking industry. Myril Hoag died in High Springs, Fla., on July 28, 1971.

RAY ROHWER

Ray Arthur Rohwer was born in Dixon, Calif., on June 5, 1895. The 5-foot-9, 165-pounder was a left-hander and had a professional baseball career, primarily as an outfielder, that spanned 11 years. Rohwer signed up for military service during World War I, but didn't serve until 1919. In 1920 he attended the University of California, Berkeley.

Rohwer began his professional baseball career in the outfield for the Pittsburgh Pirates in 1921 and got into 30 games, hitting .250. In 1922 his game improved, and he got into 53 games, hitting .295 with three home runs.

Rohwer became a regular with the Seattle Indians (Pacific Coast League) in 1923, playing in 179 games, hitting .325. He also led the league with 394 total bases and 37 home runs (back then, this was a lot!). Rohwer had another banner year in 1924 as he played in 176 games, hit .325 again, led the league in total bases again with 380, hit 33 home runs and led the league with 155 RBIs. He also led the Indians to the PCL Championship that year and was a teammate of "Brick" Eldred's.

In 1925 Rohwer had another stellar year, this time for the Portland Beavers (PCL). He played in 177 games, hit .334, and led the league in total bases with 396, RBIs with 153 and home runs with 40! He started with the Beavers in 1926, but had an off year and was traded to his hometown (or at least home area) Sacramento Senators. Between the Beavers and Senators, he played in 168 games, hitting only .254, but still had 28 home runs and 107 RBIs.

For the next five years, Rohwer was a regular for the Senators and a fan favorite. In 1927, he hit .334 in 133 games with 95 RBIs. From 1928 through 1930, he averaged 138 games a year and .279 in hitting. In 1931, Ray was 36, and played his last year in professional baseball. He did get into 110 games with a .247 batting average. He died in Davis, Calif. on Jan. 24, 1988.

EARL "WHITEY" SHEELY

Earl Homer "Whitey" Sheely was born on Feb. 12, 1893, in Bushnell, Ill., and was raised in Spokane, Wash., where he went to North Central High School. The 6-foot-4, 200-pound right-hander began his professional baseball career in 1911 with a short three-game stay with the Spokane Indians (Northwestern League). In 1912 Sheely got into eight games with the Vancouver Champions (NWL). "Whitey" became a regular (119 games) with the 1913 Walla Walla Bears (Western Tri-State League), hitting .212. In 1914, Sheely played most of the season, 93 games, with Walla Walla, but also got into five games with the Seattle Giants (NWL).

In 1915 Sheely hit .296 in 157 games at first base for the Spokane Indians.

He started the 1916 season with the Indians again, but finished with the Salt Lake City Bees (PCL). Sheely was a star first baseman for the Bees from 1916 through 1920, never batting below .300, averaging .325 over the five years, and winning the PCL batting championship in 1920 with a .371 average.

Sheely's performance with Salt Lake City earned him an opportunity with the Chicago White Sox. He played with them from 1921 to 1927, posting a .304 batting average for the seven years he was in the Windy City. Many still consider him one of the ChiSox's finest first basemen.

After he turned 35, Sheely's batting average dipped, and in 1928 he found himself back in the Pacific

Author's Collection

Coast League, this time with the Sacramento Senators. That year, he had a hefty .381 batting average, leading the team to the second-half championship, and found himself heading back up to the majors with the Pittsburgh Pirates for the 1929 season. In spite of a very respectable .293 batting average, age caught up with him and he was back in the PCL with the San Francisco Seals for the 1930 season. He had a stellar year with the bat, hitting a PCL-leading .403, and again, returned to the majors for the 1931 season, this time with the Boston Braves. He had a good season with the Braves, but he was off his lifetime major league average of an even .300, hitting only .273 in what would be his last trip to the majors.

Author's Collection

Sheely spent the next three years in the PCL with the Los Angeles Angels, the Portland Beavers and the Seattle Rainiers, and averaged .328 from 1932 to 1934. After his retirement from playing in 1934, he was a baseball coach at Gonzaga University in Spokane, Wash., and at St. Mary's College in Moraga, Calif. He also scouted for the Boston Red Sox.

From 1944 to 1946, Sheely was a popular manager of the Solons with a 265-270 record (.495). According to the Solons' front office, Sheely was a "smart baseball man, grounded in all phases of the game and particularly good in handling men." In the off-season, he was a great fishing and hunting pal of "Buddy" Ryan's. In 1946, Emil Sick, owner of the Seattle Rainiers, hired Sheely as the team's general manager, a job he held for six years.

Earl Sheely was a first baseman in the PCL for 10 years, had a .342 batting average and is a member of the PCL Hall of Fame. In 1977, he was elected into the St. Mary's College (Moraga, Calif.) Athletic Hall of Fame. He died in Seattle, Wash., on Sept. 16, 1952.

Tony Freitas (Author's Collection)

ANTONIO "TONY" FREITAS

Antonio Freitas was born in Mill Valley, Calif., on May 5, 1908. Legend has it that he learned to pitch by throwing rocks at gophers on his father's farm. He began playing organized baseball at Tamalpais Union High School. The 5-foot-8, 165-pounder threw left and batted right, and had a 26-year professional baseball career from 1928 through 1953. He attributed his pitching success to control, the curveball and the change-up, a slow pitch mixed in with fastballs designed to fool the batter.

Freitas was playing sandlot games in Mill Valley in 1928 when he caught the attention of the Sacramento Senators. Manager "Buddy" Ryan invited him to spring training, the Senators liked what they saw, signed him and sent him to the Phoenix Senators (Arizona State League) for the 1928 season.

He began the 1929 season pitching for the Globe Bears (ASL), but later in the season moved up to the Senators and appeared in 18 games.

In 1930, Freitas posted a 19-6 record for the Senators and played in the first ever Pacific Coast League night game on June 10, 1930, at Sacramento's Moreing Field. Five years later, on May 23,1935, he was with the Cincinnati Reds at Crosley Field when they played the very first major league game at night.

In 1931 Freitas posted a 19-13 record for the Senators, but probably got more attention that year for an incident involving his 1929 Ford Model A. He was driving from Marin County to Sacramento when he reportedly got the car up to 56 mph and was subsequently jailed for speeding! Manager "Buddy" Ryan convinced the judge to release Freitas so he could pitch in a game against the San Francisco Mission Reds. After posting a 5-3 win, Freitas returned to Marin to finish his five-day sentence.

In 1932, Freitas married Lillian Armstrong of Fresno. He started the 1932 season with the Senators, appearing in 11 games with a 6-4 record. On his 24th birthday, May 5, 1932, Freitas pitched a no-hitter against the Oakland Oaks (PCL).

Later in the 1932 season, Freitas moved up to pitch for the Philadelphia Athletics (American League) under legendary manager Connie Mack. He finished his rookie season with a 12-5 record. His teammates that year included Mickey Cochrane, Jimmie Foxx, Lefty Grove and Al Simmons. During that year he also played against a host of American League stars including Yankees Lou Gehrig and Babe Ruth. Tony Salin recounts Freitas' brush with Ruth in his book, *Baseball's Forgotten Heroes*, published in 1999.

"I looked at Ruth at the plate and couldn't believe I was seeing him," Freitas said. And when Ruth struck out, "The fans gave me a big hand and Ruth doffed his cap — doffed his cap to the rookie on the mound."

In 1933 Freitas got off to a bad start and was sent to the Portland Beavers (PCL) where he completed the season with a 4-7 record. He began 1934 with the St. Paul Saints (American Association) and ended up with the Cincinnati Reds under manager Charlie Dressen. He stayed through the beginning of the 1936 season. His record with the Reds during those three years was 11-24, and Freitas ended up finishing the 1936 season with the Columbus (Ohio) Senators (American Association), going 10-8.

The Solons were a top farm club for the St. Louis Cardinals from 1936 to 1944. Before the 1937 season, Freitas worked out a deal with Branch Rickey, the Cardinals' general manager, so he could come back to Sacramento. Freitas thrived when playing at "home," and from 1937 through 1942 he had six 20-win seasons.

The highlight of Freitas' career was at the end of the 1942 season when Sacramento won its first PCL championship. The Los Angeles Angels came to town with a two-game lead over the Solons for a season ending with a seven-game series. The Solons lost the first two games, but won the next three. That left them one game back of the Angels with only a doubleheader to go. In the first game, the Solons came back from a 5-0 deficit to take a 7-5 lead into the ninth. Freitas came into the game in relief and retired the side one, two, three! The Angels and Solons were then tied for the

Author's Collection

PCL lead with one game to go. Pepper Martin, the Solons' manager, decided that Freitas was warmed up and sent him in to start the second game. Freitas became a Sacramento baseball legend when he won the game, and the Pacific Coast League championship, on a 5-1 four-hitter!

It would be 61 long years until 2003, when the Sacramento River Cats would again claim the PCL pennant for Sacramento.

From 1943 to 1945 Freitas served in the U.S. Air Force. When he returned to the Solons after the war, he was still a very popular player, but at 38, he was not the pitcher he had been. From 1946 to 1949 he went 45-52. Freitas began the 1950 season with Sacramento, but after only nine games, he retired from the Solons and the PCL.

But he missed baseball, so later in 1950 he joined the Modesto Reds (California League), and had two very successful seasons posting 20-6 and 25-9 records.

Freitas was with the Stockton Ports (California League) in 1952 and 1953, where he went 18-13 and 22-9. He pitched his last season in 1953 when he was 45. At the end of the season, the fans gave him a brand new car on "Tony Freitas Day," and he responded by striking out the last three batters.

Freitas managed the Solons for part of 1954 and through 1955, but was not happy in the role. His record was 105-134 (.439). His coach was his old friend and teammate "Dolph" Camilli.

Freitas' 342 minor-league win record is the best ever achieved by a left-hander. He pitched for 16 years in the PCL, had nine 20-win seasons, a lifetime ERA of 3.11, was inducted into the PCL Hall of Fame in 2003 and was later named to the PCL All-Century Team (1903-57). Freitas is a member of the Sacramento Athletic Hall of Fame. He died in Orangevale, Calif., on March 13, 1994.

What a Lift

Tony Freitas was a Pacific Coast League Hall of Famer, a Sacramento legend in his own time, a true gentleman and an all-around great guy. When Sacramento baseball fan Zak Ford was a teenager in the mid-1990s, he had the good fortune to meet and interview Freitas. After the interview ended, Freitas found out that Ford had taken a long and circuitous bus ride to get to his house. So Freitas graciously drove the young writer home. That day is one of Ford's favorite baseball moments of all time.

"LARRY" GILLICK

George Lawrence "Larry" Gillick was born in Amador County, Calif., on July 25, 1909. He grew up in Sacramento, played some semi-professional baseball in California in 1928, and then went on to a six-year career with

Coast
League
GILLICK
Sacramento

the Pacific Coast League.

Gillick began his professional career with the San Diego Aces (California State League) in 1929, posting a 7-9 record. Later that year he got into 20 games with the Sacramento Senators, going 3-5. In 1930 he appeared in 23 games with the Globe Bears (Arizona State League) and in two games with the Senators. From 1931 through 1933, Gillick was a regular for the Senators with a 29-33 record over the three-years. He finished his PCL career with Oakland in 1934, getting into eight games with a 3-1 record. He died in Long Beach, Calif., on Oct. 20, 1988.

Gillick's son Pat was born in Northern California and played baseball at the University of Southern California. Pat Gillick was also a pitcher in the minor leagues for six years and was general manager of several major league teams after his playing career. As of this writing, Pat Gillick is general manager of the Philadelphia Phillies.

FRANK DEMAREE

Joseph Frank DeMaree was born in Winters, Calif., on June 10, 1910. Demaree roamed the outfield for six years in the Pacific Coast League with a .332 batting average, and for 12 years in the major leagues with a .299 batting average.

DeMaree was a star athlete in high school, played semi-pro ball for Marysville in the Sacramento Valley League, and was signed by the Sacramento Senators in 1930. The local favorite played for the Senators through the 1932 season, until Lew Moreing cashed in on his star outfielder and sold him to the Chicago Cubs.

DeMaree appeared in only 17 games during the regular season with the Cubs, but was fortunate enough to appear in two games of the 1932 World

COAST
LEAGUE
DEMAREE
SACRAMENTO

Author's Collection

Series against the New York Yankees. The Yankees won in four games and the series is largely remembered for Babe Ruth's "called shot" home run in game three, but DeMaree hit a home run in game four. Other Sacramentans who played in that series were: Stan Hack (Cubs) and Myril Hoag (Yankees).

DeMaree had a good 1933 season, but Cubs management decided he could benefit from another year in the minors and sent him to the Los Angeles Angels for the 1934 season. The 1934 PCL Champion Angels are considered one of the best PCL clubs ever, and DeMaree had an outstanding year with them. He had a .383 batting average, 173 RBIs, 45 home runs and was named the PCL's Most Valuable Player.

He returned to the Cubs in 1935 and made a reputation for himself as a slugger. He appeared in six games in the 1935 World Series, but the championship went to the Detroit Tigers. He hit .350 in 1936, was an All-Star that year and again in 1937. In 1938 he played in his third World Series with the Cubs (along with fellow Sacramentans Joe Marty and Stan Hack), but he was in only three games. The Yankees won in four.

DeMaree was traded to the New York Giants for the 1939 season, and he hit over .300 for two seasons. He spent most of the 1941 season and all of the 1942 season with the Boston Braves, but his average slipped into the lower .200s, and he found himself with the St. Louis Cardinals for the 1943 season. The Cardinals used him sparingly, and he was not a factor in the Cardinals' World Series loss to the Yankees. DeMaree began the 1944 season with the crosstown St. Louis Browns as a utility player. He appeared in only 16 games for the Browns and finished the 1944 season back in the PCL as a Portland Beaver. DeMaree made a comeback in 1945, and led the Beavers to the PCL Championship, hitting .304 along the way.

DeMaree managed the Fresno Cardinals (California League) in 1947 and was a player-manager in 1950 for the San Bernardino Pioneers (Sunset League). He later scouted for the Chicago White Sox. DeMaree's wife's name was Nadine. When he died in Los Angeles on Aug. 30, 1958, he was employed by United Artists Studios.

HENRY "HANK" STEINBACHER

Henry John "Hank," "Harry" Steinbacher was born in Sacramento on March 22, 1913. The 5-foot-11, 180-pounder batted left and threw right, and enjoyed a nine-year Pacific Coast League career, and a three-year career in the major leagues.

Lew Moreing signed Steinbacher out of Sacramento High School. He played for the Sacramento Senators from 1930 through 1935, and became a regular in the outfield, averaging .309 during those six seasons.

In 1936 and 1937 Steinbacher appeared in 258 games for the St. Paul Saints (American Association), hitting .333. From 1937 through 1939, he was with the Chicago White Sox, hitting .331 in 1938. From 1940 through 1942, "Hank" was a Toledo (Ohio) Mudhen, and averaged .277 at the plate. From 1943 through 1945, he played for the San Francisco Seals (PCL) averaging .286. His lifetime PCL batting average was .304.

In 1947, after returning from service in World War II, Steinbacher joined the Sacramento Police Department, retiring in 1966. He died in Sacramento on April 3, 1977.

ELWOOD "KETTLE" WIRTS

Elwood Vernon "Kettle" Wirts was born in Consumne, Calif., on Oct. 31, 1897. He attended St. Mary's College in Moraga, Calif., and had a 13-year professional baseball career, including four years in the National League and six in the Pacific Coast League. "Kettle" was a 5-foot-11, 170-pounder who batted and threw right, and signed his first professional baseball contract in 1918 with the Spokane Indians (Northwestern League). He played in 1919 in a Canadian league and spent part of the 1920 season with the Dallas Steers (Texas League).

The Chicago Cubs bought his contract in 1921, and he was a Cubbie through the 1923 season. In 1924 he moved across town to the Chicago White Sox. His major league career was spent primarily as a bench player and his lifetime batting average was .163. He did, however, get some playing time against such old-time greats as Ty Cobb and Rogers Hornsby, and one of his

Author's Collection

COAST
LEAGUE
WIRTS
SACRAMENTO

greatest thrills was catching for famed pitcher Grover Cleveland Alexander.

Wirts played for the Sacramento Senators from 1930 to 1935, with a batting average of .265. He managed the team for part of the 1935 season.

After retiring from the Senators, he went into wine distribution and real estate. He and his wife, Ines, had two children: Mary Jane and Jack. Wirts died in Sacramento on July 12, 1968.

STANLEY HACK

Stanley Canfield Hack was born in Sacramento on Dec. 6, 1909. He graduated from Sacramento High School and was a star ballplayer in the Sacramento Winter League. The 6-foot 170-pounder batted with his left hand and threw with his right.

In 1931 Hack came to the attention of "Buddy" Ryan, the Sacramento Senators' manager, and he was invited to spring training. Hack took two weeks' vacation from his job as a bank teller at the Bank of America at Eighth and J streets and played well enough to make the club as a bench player. When "Lennie" Backer was injured in April, Hack took over at third base, batting .352 and scoring 128 runs. At the end of the season Lew Moreing grabbed an opportunity to make some money and sold Hack to the Chicago Cubs for $42,500.

Hack played third base for the Chicago Cubs from 1932 through 1947. During this 16-year playing career, he batted .301 in 1,836 games. He was a five-time All-Star and played in four World Series championships: 1932, 1935, 1938 and 1945. In 1938, Sacramentans Joe Marty and Frank Demaree were also on the team. Hack averaged .348 during those four World Series games, but unfortunately, the Cubs didn't win a championship. Hack led the National League in stolen bases in 1938 and 1939 and in hits in 1940 and 1941.

After the 1947 season, Hack managed in the Cubs' farm system and was manager of the Los Angeles Angles (PCL) for the 1951, 1952 and 1953

Author's Collection

seasons. From 1954 through 1956 Hack was back managing the Cubs, and then for part of the 1958 season he managed the St. Louis Cardinals. After he retired from baseball, he became a restaurant owner.

Hack had five children: Stanley Jr., Stanford, David, Barbara and Beverly. In his book, *Pacific Coast League Stars: Ninety Who Made it in the Majors, 1903-1957*, John Spalding called Hack "the best player ever to come out of Sacramento." Hack is a member of the Sacramento Athletic Hall of Fame, and there are those who believe he belongs in the MLB Hall of Fame, including Jim Vitti, author of *The Cubs on Catalina*. Stanley Hack died in Dixon, Ill., on Dec. 15, 1979.

ALEXANDER "KAMPY" KAMPOURIS

Alexander William "Kampy" Kampouris was born in Sacramento on Nov. 13, 1912. He starred in football and baseball at Sacramento High School and went to Sacramento City College. After excelling in Sacramento Winter League ball in 1931, Lew Moreing signed "Kampy" to play for the Sacramento Senators.

The 5-foot-8, 160-pound right-hander was the regular second baseman for the Senators from 1932 to 1934, posting a .304 batting average in 1933. In 1934, when "Kampy's" baseball skills came to the attention of the National League's Cincinnati Reds, Moreing sold his contract, as he had done with other players, so the Senators had the funds necessary to keep on playing.

Kampouris was the Reds' regular second baseman from 1934 through part of the 1938 season. According to Diamantis Zervos' book, *Baseball's Golden Greeks*, Kampouris "became the first player of Greek descent to reach the major leagues." "Kampy" was a roommate of future Solons and MLB Hall-of-Famer Ernie Lombardi, and some say Kampouris was the best defensive second baseman of his era. On May 9, 1937, he hit three consecutive home runs on three different pitchers in one game! He was later voted to the Reds' "All Time" team. In June 1938, he was traded to the New York Giants for Wally Berger.

Kampouris was a regular during the 1938 season, and was very popular with the large turnout of Greek fans at New York Giants games. He was used sparingly during the 1939 season, and after that season the New York Yankees bought his contract. In 1940, he was with the Yankees' farm club, the Newark Bears (International League), and in 1941, he was with the Brooklyn Dodgers' farm club, the Montreal Royals (International League). From 1942 through 1943 he was with the Dodgers but seldom played.

Kampouris finished his MLB career in 1943, playing in 51 games with the Washington Senators and ending with a lifetime MLB batting average of .243. In 1944 and 1945, he was in the U.S. Air Force.

In 1946, after his service in World War II, Kampouris returned home to Sacramento and played second base for the Solons through the 1948 season. His last year in professional baseball was 1948, and he retired with a lifetime PCL batting average of .277. He was later elected into the Sacramento Athletic Hall of Fame.

After he retired from baseball, Kampouris went to work for the city Parks and Recreation Department, and later the Sacramento County Marshal's Office. He and his wife, Della, raised their children, Patricia and Alexander, in Sacramento's Land Park. Alexander Kampouris died in Sacramento on May 29, 1993.

Author's Collection

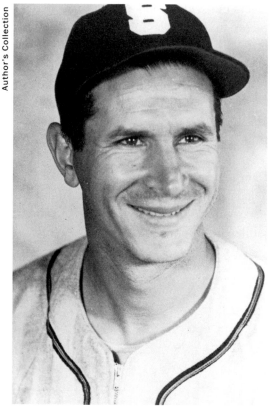

"MANNY" SALVO

Manuel "Manny" Salvo was born in Sacramento on June 30, 1913. The 6-foot-4, 200-pound right-hander played in various semi-pro leagues in the Sacramento area, and had an 18-year professional career as a pitcher, including five years in the majors and 12 in the Pacific Coast League.

Salvo began his career in 1931, getting into 12 games for the Phoenix Senators (Arizona-Texas League). The Sacramento Senators signed him in 1932 and he pitched for them through the 1935 season with a combined 38-50 record.

In 1936 he went to spring training with the American League's Boston Red Sox, but was traded to the San Diego Padres (PCL) in a deal that included Bobby Doerr. From 1936 through 1938, Salvo was a Padre and had a terrific 56-34 record. During his stay he got into a fight with San Francisco Seals' (PCL) manager Lefty O'Doul over close pitches.

In 1937 the Padres won the Governor's Cup and the PCL championship. Salvo's performance with the Padres earned him a position with the New York Giants for the 1939 season.

After going 4-10 for the Giants, he was traded in 1940 to the Boston Braves where he pitched though the 1943 season and finished his MLB career at 33 and 50. Salvo was picked up by the Oakland Oaks (PCL) in 1944 and had an outstanding year with them with an 18-7 record and a 2.14 ERA. In 1945 he served his country in the military. In 1946 Salvo returned to the Padres and pitched for them partway through the 1948 season. Salvo returned home and pitched for the Solons from 1948 through 1949, retiring from baseball after the 1949 season. He died in Vallejo, Calif., on Feb. 7, 1997.

WILLIAM "BILL" SALKELD

William Franklin Salkeld was born in Pocatello, Idaho, on March 8, 1917. The 5-foot-10, 190-pounder batted left and threw right. He was a catcher at Sacramento High School, and in 1934 at 17, signed a contract with the Sacramento Senators, beginning what would be an 18-year professional baseball career.

Salkeld played for the Senators from 1934 to 1935, appearing in 200 games with a .258 batting average. At the end of the 1935 season, he was traded to the San Francisco Seals (PCL).

Because of injuries, in 1936 Salkeld appeared in only 69 Seals games (he was a teammate of Joe Marty's), and he missed all of the 1937 and 1938 seasons. In 1939, he got into 18 Seals games and 102 Tucson Cowboys (Arizona-Texas League) games, and had Charley Schanz as a teammate.

From 1940 though 1944, Salkeld was a regular with the San Diego Padres (PCL) hitting .264. From 1945 through 1947, he appeared in 211 Pittsburgh Pirates games, hitting .293 for them. From 1948 through 1949, he caught in 144 Boston Braves games, hitting .247. He also was on the Braves team that lost to the Cleveland Indians in the 1948 World Series.

In 1950 Salkeld got into one Chicago White Sox game and 104 games with the Seattle Rainiers (PCL). He finished his career in 1951 with 32 games for the Portland Beavers (PCL). He died in Los Angeles on April 22, 1967.

ARTHUR "ART" GARIBALDI

Arthur "Art" Edward Garibaldi was born in San Francisco on Aug. 21, 1907. The 5-foot-8, 165-pound right-hander played infield and had a professional baseball career that spanned 12 years.

Garibaldi began his career with the San Francisco Seals (PCL) and was a regular from 1931 through 1935, hitting .301. His success earned him a trip to St. Louis, Mo., with the Cardinals in 1936. Later in the 1936 season, Garibaldi

was sent to the Solons where he hit .326. He also played the 1937 season for the Solons, batting in 106 runs and achieving a .327 average.

In 1938 Garibaldi was with the Columbus Senators (American Association), but he was back with the Solons for the 1939 season, hitting .251. A Solons' game program called him "the best third baseman in the league," and said "... Garibaldi's hitting has always been ... consistent and timely," and that he also possessed "speed and base-stealing knowledge."

Splitting the 1940 season between the Solons and the San Diego Padres (PCL), again hitting .251, Garibaldi was with the Padres in 1941, and finished his career with them in 1942. One of the high points of his career was rooming with Cards' pitcher "Dizzy" Dean. After baseball Garibaldi became a bartender at Sacramento's Pal's Club, where the motto was, "You Are a Stranger But Once." Garibaldi died in Sacramento on Oct. 19, 1967.

WILLIAM "BILL" SCHMIDT

William "Berkeley Bill" Schmidt was born in Sacramento on Nov. 13, 1912. The 6-foot-2, 190-pound right-hander played semi-professional ball in Berkeley, Calif., in 1932 and later had a 10-year professional baseball career.

In 1933 "Berkeley Bill" pitched in 24 games for the Rock Island (Ill.) Islanders (Mississippi Valley League) and compiled a 10-6 record. From 1934 through 1936, he pitched 114 games for the Atlanta (Ga.) Crackers (Southern Association) with a three-year record of 44-30.

Schmidt was a regular with the Solons from 1937 through the 1942 championship year, appearing in 224 games with an 84-74 record, a 3.31 ERA, 21 wins in 1938 and 20 in 1939. He died in Eureka, Calif., on Sept. 11, 1996.

Marguerite Pintar Collection

JOHN PINTAR

John Pintar was born in McGill, Nev., on Aug. 6, 1913. He attended the University of San Francisco on a basketball and track scholarship and, upon graduating in 1936, signed a baseball contract with the San Francisco Missions (Pacific Coast League). The 6-foot-1, 170-pound right-hander began his playing career in 1936 with the Muskogee (Okla.) Tigers (Western Association), where he had a 12-20 record with a 4.54 ERA in 37 appearances.

In 1937 Pintar pitched in 33 games for the Bartlesville (Okla.) Blues (Western Association), going 11-18 with a 4.13 ERA. Pintar had very good pitching years in 1938 and 1939 with the Wenatchee Chiefs (Western International League) with 11-9 and 3.12 ERA and 19-10 and 3.47 ERA records, respectively.

Pintar pitched in 32 games in 1940 for the Dallas Rebels (Texas League) with an 11-9 record and a 2.77 ERA. In 1941, Pintar went 13-11 with a 3.08 ERA for the Houston Buffalos (Texas League).

Pintar pitched for the Solons from 1942 through 1946, appearing in 96 games with a 14-33 record. He had a 3-0 record with a 3.63 ERA for the 1942 PCL Champion Solons.

Pintar closed out his professional career in 1946 with the Bremerton (Wash.) Bluejackets (WIL). One of his great baseball memories was arguing with Branch Rickey, the St. Louis Cardinals' general manager, over a $600 baseball contract. Rickey won the argument, but Pintar signed with the Cardinals' organization and went to the Wenatchee Chiefs, the Solons' farm team.

John and Marguerite Pintar married in 1936 and had three children: John, Donn and Marlene. After baseball, Pintar stayed in Sacramento, went into the trucking business, worked as an inspector at Aerojet and as a custodian at Hiram Johnson High School. He retired in 1975. He was an avid golfer, shooting an 84 when he was 86. He died in Sacramento on Oct. 29, 2002.

Numbers

When I was going through John Pintar's baseball mementoes, I found a letter he had written to the Boston Braves, late in his baseball career, asking for a tryout. He listed his experience and said that he was in his late 20s. I was initially taken aback because I knew he was in his 30s at the time, but then I realized that like many other ballplayers he had "hedged" his age and grabbed a chance to prove his ability.

VERNAL "NIPPY" JONES

Vernal Leroy "Nippy" Jones was born in Los Angeles on June 29, 1925. The 6-foot-1, 185-pound right-hander spent eight years with the Solons and eight years in the major leagues.

Jones was signed right out of high school and played first and second base for the Solons in 1943, batting .304. He was in the Marine Corps from late 1943 to early 1946.

In 1946, Jones was a member of the St. Louis Cardinals' farm club, the Rochester, N.Y., Red Wings (International League). Although he batted .344 that year, he was edged out for the league batting title by Jackie Robinson, who batted .349. "Nippy" was called up to the Cardinals late in the season, hitting .333 in 16 games and making one appearance in the 1946 World Series, which the Cardinals won. (He continued with the Cardinals through the 1951 season.) In 1949 he had his best year when he hit .300 batting cleanup behind Stan Musial. That was the same year he sustained a back injury that affected his career. He spent part of the 1952 season with the Phillies.

Jones returned to the Solons from 1953 to 1957, when he averaged .298 and was one of the most popular Solons players ever. *Sacramento Bee* sports editor Bill Conlin once wrote that Jones might have been Sacramento's most popular player.

His consistent performance earned him an opportunity to play first base with the Milwaukee Braves in 1957. He is, perhaps, best remembered for the "shoe polish" incident in the 1957 World Series. Jones batted in the bottom of the 10th inning in the fourth game, with the Braves trailing the New York Yankees 5-4. It appeared he avoided a wild pitch, but he pointed to a polish smudge on the ball and was awarded first base. The Braves rallied behind Eddie Mathews' three-run home run to win the game 7-5 and went on to win the World Series in seven games.

In 1957, Jones settled in Sacramento, where he and his wife, Nora, raised their daughters Debra, Dianne, Cheryl and Cindi. He returned to the Solons for the

Sacramento Bee 1947 - SAMCC

1957 and 1958 seasons, and played for the Portland Beavers (PCL) in 1960.

After he retired from baseball, Jones worked in public relations and in the title insurance business, then he became a professional fishing guide on the Sacramento River. He died in Sacramento on Oct. 3, 1995.

FRANK BOWA

Frank Bowa was born in Sacramento on Oct. 2, 1924. The 5-foot-10, 155-pound right-hander appeared in seven games at second and third bases for the Solons in 1944. Paul Bowa was his brother. He died in Sacramento on March 7, 1979.

PAUL BOWA

Paul Bowa was born in Sacramento on Aug. 28, 1918. In 1944, the 5-foot-9, 165-pound right-hander appeared in 72 games as a middle infielder for the Solons. He later managed the Duluth Dukes, a St. Louis Cardinals' farm club (Northern League). Paul coached and managed both Little League and American Legion teams in Sacramento and mentored his grandson, major leaguer Nick Johnson. His son is former manager and MLB star Larry Bowa. Paul Bowa died in Sacramento on Aug. 22, 1994.

The Dad
Paul Bowa instilled the love of baseball and a never-quit attitude in son Larry that contributed to Larry's decades-long success as a major league player, coach and manager.

Gold on the Diamond

PERRY "TED" GREENHALGH

Perry Theodore "Ted" Greenhalgh was born in McCloud, Calif., on Dec. 1, 1921. The 5-foot-8, 160-pound right-hander played the outfield for the Solons from 1944 through 1946. In 1944, Greenhalgh appeared in 52 games hitting .261; in 1945, 94 games hitting .295; and in 1946, 48 games hitting .211. He died in Orangevale, Calif., on Aug. 25, 1986.

LILIO MARCUCCI

Lilio Robert Marcucci was born in Bozzano, Italy, on May 5, 1922. The 5-foot-9, 200-pound right-hander played baseball at Mission High School in San Francisco and attended San Jose State College.

Marcucci caught regularly for the Solons from 1944 though 1946, appearing in 336 games with a .267 batting average. From 1947 through 1948, he was a regular for the Stockton Ports (California League), where he averaged .311.

In 1949, he hit .413 for the Reno (Nev.) Silver Sox (Sunset League), and in 1950 he hit .367 for the Idaho Falls Russetts (Pioneer League).

In 1951 Marcucci got into 39 games with the Portland Beavers (PCL) and 59 games for the Victoria Athletics (Western International League). He was back with Victoria in 1952, but he got into only 47 games hitting .288. His final year of professional baseball was in 1953 when he hit .285 for the Modesto Reds (California League). He died in Sacramento on March 22, 2002.

CURTIS "CURT" SCHMIDT

Curtis William "Curt" Schmidt was born in Sacramento on Jan. 1, 1918. The 6-foot-2, 185-pound right-hander attended Santa Clara College, played semi-professional baseball for the semi-pro Carmichael Firemen in Sacramento in 1938, and had a nine-year professional baseball career, primarily as an outfielder.

In 1939 Schmidt played in the outfield in a combined 43 games for the Arizona-Texas

League's El Paso Texans and Tucson Cowboys. In 1940 he was in the outfield for 10 games split between the Big Springs (Texas) Barons and the Midland Cowboys, both in the West Texas-New Mexico League. From 1941 through 1944, he was out of organized baseball, presumably spending part of this time in military service.

Schmidt was back in 1945, appearing in 38 PCL games at third base and in the outfield for the Portland Beavers and the Solons. In 1946 the Solons sent him to the Wenatchee Chiefs (Western International League), where he played third base and worked on his hitting. Later that year he was in the outfield for the Boise Pilots (Pioneer League), hitting .251.

In 1947 Schmidt was again out of organized baseball, but in 1948 he played briefly with the Duluth Dukes (Northern League). In 1949 he got into 55 games for the Willows Cardinals (Far West League), hitting .331. He was out of organized baseball again in 1950.

In 1951 Schmidt was back in, splitting 49 games between the Vancouver Capilanos and the Salem Senators in the Western International League. In 1952 he was with Salem and with Wenatchee for a total of 31 games. He spent the last part of the season in Texas, playing 17 games for the Amarillo Gold Sox (West Texas-New Mexico League), and the Odessa Oilers (Longhorn League). His final year of professional baseball was 1953 with the Idaho Falls Russets (Pioneer League). Curtis Schmidt died in Sacramento on Jan. 26, 1996.

Helluva Singer When I attended Sacramento's McClatchy High School in the 1960s, Curtis Schmidt was on the athletic staff. Bill Conlin, a sports editor for The Sacramento Bee, said in a story on Feb. 25, 1996, that Schmidt "was a particular favorite of Lefty O'Doul's, the San Francisco Seals manager, for his secondary skills as a piano-bar vocalist."

ED FITZ GERALD

Edward Raymond Fitz Gerald was born in Santa Ynez, Calif., on May 21, 1924, and starred in baseball and basketball in high school in his hometown. The 6-foot, 180-pound right-hander's baseball talent earned him a scholarship to St. Mary's College in Moraga, Calif., where he played for Earl Sheely, who at that time was the baseball coach. Fitz Gerald's college career ended when he was drafted into the U.S. Army in 1943. He served in the Aleutian Islands and later in Germany where, as it says on his 1947 Signal Gasoline baseball card, "He once captured two Germans single-handedly on the Rhine."

Ed Fitz Gerald (Joe Benetti, photographer; Author's Collection)

After World War II, Earl Sheely remembered Fitz Gerald and signed him to a Solons contract in 1946. Fitz Gerald began his professional baseball career that year with the Solons' farm club, the Wenatchee Chiefs (Western International League), under "Buddy" Ryan. There, he caught in 91 games, hitting .338. He also got into 11 Solons games that year. One of the Solons' programs from that time described Fitz Gerald as "fast and hits a long ball. He handles pitchers in workmanlike fashion, and the Solons moundsmen are all praises for his work behind the log."

In 1947 Fitz Gerald became the Solons starting catcher, hitting .363. The same program described him as "one of the best hitters in the Pacific Coast League ... and one of the finest young receivers to appear in recent years."

From 1948 through 1953, Fitz Gerald appeared in 295 games for the Pittsburgh Pirates, where he was a teammate of Wally Westlake. From 1953 through 1959, he appeared in 463 games for the American League's Washington (D.C.) Senators, and in 1959 he appeared in 49 games for the Cleveland Indians. He finished his playing career with a lifetime MLB batting average of .260.

Fitz Gerald coached in the majors for a few years starting in 1960 under the Cleveland Indians' manager Joe Gordon. In the mid-1960s, he managed the Fresno Giants, where Bobby Bonds, the future San Francisco Giants star, was among his protégés. In the late 1960s, Fitz Gerald coached for the Kansas City A's, again with Joe Gordon, and said recently in an interview that he was "the second person fired by Charlie Finley."

After he left baseball, Fitz Gerald worked for the California State Printing Plant in Sacramento. He said in a recent interview that he "owes a lot of his baseball success to Earl Sheely." He is a member of the Sacramento Athletic Hall of Fame.

JOSEPH MARTY

Joseph "Joe" Anton Marty was born at 522 M St., Sacramento, on Sept. 1, 1913. His father, Anton Joseph Marty, emigrated from Switzerland to San Francisco and was a baker there until the 1906 earthquake, when he was so unnerved he moved to Sacramento. Anton Marty was a bartender in Charley Holdener's saloon, in what is now Old Sacramento. When Holdener retired, Marty bought the business and turned it into the William Tell Bar and Restaurant. The restaurant was said to have had the best Limburger cheese in town.

Joe Marty was involved in sports at Sacramento's Christian Brothers High School until he graduated in 1931. The CBS baseball field is now named for him. He attended St. Mary's College in Moraga, Calif., on a sports scholarship and became a star baseball, football, and basketball player.

The 6-foot, 180-pound right-hander was an outfielder for 10 Pacific Coast League seasons with a lifetime PCL batting average of .309. From 1934 to 1936 Marty played for the San Francisco Seals, often alongside Joe DiMaggio and Lefty O'Doul. In a story published in *The Sacramento Bee* on Sept. 1, 1994, former sports editor Bill Conlin said, "Marty then was so fleet afoot and so defensively skilled that he played center field on this San Francisco Seals team of 1935, forcing DiMag (Joe DiMaggio) into right field. Manager O'Doul played left field, a concession to his failing arm." Conlin asserted that this may have been the Pacific Coast League's greatest outfield. At .359, Marty also was the 1936 PCL batting champion. His sale for $50,000 to the Chicago Cubs at the end of the 1936 season saved the financially strapped San Francisco franchise.

No Sissy Drinks

Joe Marty had a reputation for being somewhat gruff. Many Sacramentans knew Marty had a bar on Broadway called Joe Marty's, and that he often tended bar. He viewed his bar as a "man's bar" and when someone asked for a drink he thought was a "sissy drink" he would request (in what is commonly referred to as "blue language") that the patron take his business elsewhere.

Marty played for the Chicago Cubs from the 1937 to 1939 seasons, and was the first Cub to hit a home run in a night game — July 1, 1938, in Cincinnati.

In a game against the New York Giants, Marty once turned a sure double into a single when he stopped at first base to ogle movie star Tallulah Bankhead who had front-row box seats.

Marty hit .500 with a home run in the Cubs 1938 World Series against the Yankees. He was the first native Sacramentan to hit a home run in a World Series, and even though the Cubs lost, Marty out-hit Lou Gehrig, Tommy Heinrich, Joe Gordon and Joe DiMaggio! Other Sacramento-area players in the series were Chicago Cubs Frank DeMaree and Stan Hack, and Yankees Joe Gordon and Myril Hoag.

Marty played part of the 1939 season — and all of the 1940 and 1941 seasons — with the Philadelphia Phillies. In 1939, during one game he thought was a lost cause, Phillies Manager Doc Prothro decided to save his pitchers and sent Marty in. "I did not mind going to the mound because it

Joe Marty (Author's Collection)

was a shorter walk than to right field," Marty said in a *Sacramento Sports* magazine story on April 1, 1984. His lifetime MLB was .261.

Four years' military service in World War II interrupted Marty's major league career. He tried to enlist in the Marine Corps, but was rejected when they declared him color blind. He became a supply sergeant in the U.S. Army, and while he was stationed on Tinian Island in 1945, he watched the *Inola Gay* take off for Japan with its atomic bomb. Marty returned to Sacramento after the war with one of the PCL's top salaries. He was a star outfielder and slugger for the Solons from 1946 to 1952.

Joe Marty — Sacramento Solons

In 1950, Marty had starred in right field for five years, and replaced Red Kress as the Solons' manager in June. In a show of appreciation, fans presented him with a 1950 Buick Special Dynaflow at Edmonds Field's home plate. Marty loved and drove that car for 34 years. In 1974, the car had been repainted twice, and was on its third set of seat covers when local Buick dealers included Marty in their ads with the slogan: "I've been driving mine for 24 years … that's quality." Marty finished the season with a 58-77 (.430) managerial record. Joe Gordon became manager in 1951.

After the 1952 season, Marty retired from baseball and for the next three decades tended bar at Joe Marty's bar on Broadway at 15th Street. According to a story in the April 1, 1984, issue of *Sacramento Sports* magazine, he once said that his favorite teams were the Chicago Cubs "because Chicago bars never close," and the San Francisco Seals because the "ballpark was close to the Irish saloons."

Marty was elected to the Sacramento Athletic Hall of Fame. He and his wife, Elleanore, raised a son, Joseph. Joe Marty died in Sacramento on Oct. 4, 1984.

NICKOLAUS "NICK" PESUT

Nickolaus Joseph Pesut was born in DeKalb, Ill., on Dec. 31, 1920. The 6-foot-3, 225-pounder batted left and threw right and had a 10-year professional baseball career, primarily as a catcher, with a .276 lifetime batting average.

In 1940, Pesut tried out with professional ball clubs in Lubbock, Texas, and in Jonesboro, Ark. He ended up playing semi-pro ball during 1941 and most of 1942. In 1942 he got into a handful of professional games with the Duluth Dukes (Northern League).

During World War II, he served as a Marine Corps sergeant from 1943 through 1945. In 1946 he returned to professional baseball, playing in 77 games and batting .305 for the Solons' farm team, the Wenatchee Chiefs (Western International League).

He came to spring training with the Solons in 1947. His manager, Earl Sheely, was impressed saying, "(he) has been working hard in camp and shows he can handle the mask." That year Pesut appeared in 62 games for the Chiefs and 34 for the Solons. He caught in 61 games for the Solons during the 1948 season, but was back with the Chiefs in 1949.

From 1950 though 1953, Pesut played regularly for the Tri-City Braves (Kenniwick, Pasco and Richland, Wash.) in the Western International League. His final season was in 1954, when he played in 71 games for the Vancouver Capilanos (WIL) helping them win the league pennant.

After retiring from professional baseball, Pesut moved back to Sacramento and worked as a foreman for Teichert Construction. He also played on the 1955 Julius' team in Winter League baseball. His children, Michael, Steve, and

Some Kids
When I was a teenager, I lived around the corner from Nick Pesut and often hung out with his son Mike. Sometimes, I would cut across the Pesut lawn to get to the front porch and fondly remember Nick yelling at me to "stay off the grass."

Lori, went to McClatchy High School. Nickolaus Pesut died in Sacramento on Feb. 16, 1972.

JAMES "RAWHIDE" TABOR

James "Jim" Reubin "Rawhide" Tabor was born in New Hope, Ala., on Nov. 5, 1916. He was an excellent high school basketball and football player and was involved in athletics at the University of Alabama before signing with the Boston Red Sox. The 6-foot-1-, 190-pound right-hander had a 15-year professional baseball career, primarily as a third baseman.

Tabor began his career in 1937 with the Little Rock (Ark.) Travelers (Southern Association), getting into 137 games and hitting .296. In 1938 he moved up to the Minneapolis Millers (American Association), hitting .330 in 103 games. Later that season he moved up again, this time to the Boston Red Sox. Tabor became the regular third baseman for the Red Sox from 1939 through 1944, and during the first game of his first season hit a grand slam off Hall-of-Fame pitcher Bob Feller.

Late in 1944 he went into the Army to serve in World War II. He was discharged in 1946, and the Philadelphia Phillies signed him later that year. He stayed with them though the 1947 season.

In 1948 he started the season with the Los Angeles Angels (Pacific Coast League) and finished it with the Solons. In the winter of 1948, he worked on the construction crew that rebuilt Edmonds Field, which had been destroyed by fire in July. From 1949 though 1950, he was the Solons regular third baseman. He started the 1951 season with the Solons, but was later traded to the San Diego Padres (PCL) for pitcher Jess Flores. In 1952 he appeared in eight games at first base for the Portland Beavers(PCL).

After baseball, Tabor settled in Sacramento making his living in the construction business. He died in Sacramento on Aug. 22, 1953. The Bee's story about him that day called him "one of the great natural hitters of baseball."

Orval Grove
SACRAMENTO

ORVAL "ORV" GROVE

Orval Leroy "Orv" Grove was born in Mineral, Kan., on Aug. 29, 1919. The 6-foot-3, 195-pound right-handed pitcher had a four-year Pacific Coast League career, all with the Solons, and a 10-year major league career, all with the Chicago White Sox.

In 1938 Grove pitched for the Longview Cannibals (East Texas League) posting a 10-11 record. In 1939 he was with the Oklahoma City Indians (Texas League), going 8-7 with a 2.91 ERA. His fine 1939 season earned him a shot with the Chicago White Sox in 1940, and over the next 10 years, Grove appeared in 207 games for the Sox with a 63-73 record and a 3.78 ERA. He was elected to the American League All-Star team in 1944.

In 1949 Grove was acquired by the Solons and was a very popular player for the next four years. From 1949 through 1952, he pitched in 137 games with a 40-48 record and a 3.72 ERA. He died in Carmichael, Calif., on April 29, 1992.

RICHARD "RICHIE" MYERS

Richard "Richie" W. Myers was born in Sacramento on April 7, 1930. He attended and played baseball at Elk Grove High School and also played American Legion ball with Sam Kanelos. His high school teammates included Kanelos and Gene Roenspie.

The 5-foot-5, 155-pound right-hander appeared in 17 games for the Solons in 1948, five games in 1949 and 79 games in 1950. Myers also played briefly with the Twin Falls (Idaho) Cowboys (Pioneer League) in 1948 and in 145

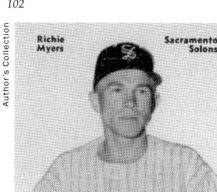

Richie
Myers

Sacramento
Solons

games with the Wenatchee Chiefs (Western International League) in 1949, hitting .301 and leading the league in triples. Myers was the regular shortstop for the 1951 Salem Senators (WIL).

From 1952 through 1955 Myers was a fan favorite as the regular shortstop for the Solons. One internal Solons' report called him a "great fielder, one of the best arms in baseball."

Myers finished his career as a member of the 1956 PCL Champion Los Angeles Angels. His lifetime PCL batting average was .254. He also played briefly with the 1956 Chicago Cubs.

SAM "GREEK" KANELOS

Samuel "Greek" Kanelos was born in Sacramento on Oct. 15, 1930. The right-handed switch-hitter played sandlot baseball in the Sacramento area and was a starter at second base for his first three years at Elk Grove High School. Among his teammates there were Gene Roenspie and "Richie" Myers. Kanelos was not eligible to play his senior year because he was already playing semi-pro ball for the Carmichael Firemen. He also was an active player in the American Legion League playing for the Florin Legion team.

Kanelos graduated from high school in 1949. The Solons signed him for the 1950 season. He went to spring training in Anaheim and was encouraged by manager Red Kress for his play at second base. He spent most of the season gaining experience with the Waterloo (Iowa) Hawks in the "Three Eye" League (which stands for the three I's in Illinois, Indiana and Iowa). At 200 games, the PCL season was longer than the Three-I season, so Kanelos was able to appear in 20 late-season games for the Solons, hitting .286. Joe Marty replaced Red Kress as manager in late 1950, and let Kanelos know that he had a good shot at becoming the Solons' starting second baseman in 1951. But, as luck would have it, Joe Marty was replaced as manager for the 1951 season by American League All-Star second-baseman Joe Gordon, who started himself at second. Kanelos was sent to the Colorado Springs Sky Sox (Western International League) for more seasoning.

Kanelos thoroughly enjoyed playing for the Solons, especially the travel along the coast from San Diego to Seattle. He said that wearing wool uniforms in Sacramento in August didn't bother him or the other players because they all loved the game and got some relief from the heat in the shade of the dugout and by putting their arms in buckets of ice water that a groundskeeper named "Smitty" would haul in for them.

Kanelos injured his thumb in the spring of 1952 and was sold to the Toronto Maple Leafs (International League). From there, he was sent to the Spokane Indians (Northwestern League) where he played mostly third base, hitting .296. He spent the 1953 season with the Edmonton Eskimos (Northwest League) playing third base and hitting in the high .200s. In 1954, Kanelos was playing with the Tri-City Braves (Kenniwick, Pasco and Richland, Wash.) in the Western International League.

After five years of professional baseball, which provided a limited income, Kanelos left for the trucking business. In the 1950s he also worked as a bartender at Old Ironsides on

Sam Kanelos Collection

10ᵗʰ and S streets and ended up as the owner in the 1970s. He still operates the bar, which has become a great pub with live music. Kanelos and his wife, Billee Jean, have four children: Sam Jr., Janell, Kim and Marla.

Kanelos says he is especially proud to have played in the March 1951 game between the Solons and the New York Yankees. (At the time, the Yankee roster included Joe DiMaggio and Mickey Mantle.) He also said that he is "happy to have played the game and made a lot of good friends."

EUGENE "GENE" ROENSPIE

Eugene "Gene" Albert Roenspie was born on Jan. 2, 1930, in Sacramento. He went to Elk Grove High School, where he pitched, played third base and had Sam Kanelos and "Richie" Myers (his across-the-street neighbor) as teammates. The 6-foot-1, 170-pounder batted and threw right-handed.

Roenspie began his professional baseball career in 1948 with the San Bernardino Pioneers (Sunset League) and was with them through the 1949 season with a 20-11 record. He appeared in three games for the 1950 Solons and also spent time that year with the Colorado Springs Sky Sox (Western League) and the Tri-City (Wash.) Braves (Western International League).

In 1951 Roenspie appeared in five games for the Solons and had a 1-0 record with a 2.25 ERA. He spent part of 1951 and all of 1952 in the U.S. Army serving his country during the Korean conflict.

During the 1953 and 1954 seasons, he was used sparingly by the Solons and appeared in only 10 games during those two years with an 0-3 record. He also spent time in 1953 with the Salem (Ore.) Senators (Western International League).

After retiring from baseball, "Gene" worked for the Coffin Redington Drug Company (later Bergen Brunswick) for 40 years. He retired in 1995.

JOSEPH "FLASH" GORDON

Joseph Lowell "Flash" Gordon was born in Los Angeles on Feb. 18, 1915. He grew up in Portland Ore., and the 5-foot-10, 180-pound right-hander was an outstanding athlete at the University of Oregon, playing both baseball and football.

In 1936 he played shortstop for the Oakland Oaks (Pacific Coast League) and batted .300. In 1937 he was with the Newark Bears, one of the New York Yankees' farm system teams. In 1938 he moved up to the Yankees, where,

Eugene Roenspie (Author's Collection)

with Frank Crosetti at shortstop, he was moved to second base replacing Tony Lazzeri.

"Flash" had a stellar major league career playing second base for the New York Yankees from 1938 to 1943 and again in 1946. He and shortstop Phil Rizzuto formed one of major league baseball's finest keystone combinations. Gordon was in the military from 1944 through 1945, was a nine-time All-Star and in 1942 was named the American League's Most Valuable Player over triple-crown champion Ted Williams. He appeared in the World Series six times, and his teams won five of the six. Many think that Gordon, who hit .500 in the 1941 World Series, would have won the World Series Most Valuable Player award, had there been such an award at the time.

Joe Gordon — Sacramento Solons

Author's Collection

When Gordon's batting average slipped to .210 in 1946, he was traded for the 1947 season to the Cleveland Indians where he stayed from 1947 to 1950.

When he was signed as manager of the Solons in 1951, Gordon started himself at second base. That year he hit .299 — 43 home runs and 136 RBIs (the two latter stats were club records). Besides playing well, Gordon was a great gate draw. In 1952, however, his home runs dropped to 16 and his average to .246. With seventh- and eighth-place finishes, he resigned as a manager and player when the season ended.

Gordon scouted for the Detroit Tigers from 1953 through 1956, then took over as manager of the San Francisco Seals, guiding them to a 1957 Pacific Coast League Championship.

From 1958 through two-thirds of the 1960 season, Gordon was manager of the Cleveland Indians. In 1960 he was involved in one of the most unusual trades in baseball history when he was traded for Detroit Tiger manager Jimmy Dykes. (In Dykes' obituary on April 15, 1978, *The New York Times* quoted his comment about the trade at the time: "I've been around baseball a long time," Dykes said, "but I've never seen anything like this.")

Gordon finished the 1960 season with the Tigers, but started the 1961 season as skipper of the Kansas City (Mo.) Athletics under Charlie O. Finley. After starting 26-33, he was let go. In 1969 he came back to manage the new

Kansas City Royals, but with a 69-93 season record, that was his only year with the club.

After baseball, Gordon became successful in real estate sales in the Sacramento area. He was an avid outdoorsman and enjoyed hunting and fishing in Northern California. He also was an excellent golfer. He and his wife, Dorothy, had two children: Joe Jr. and Judy. He later became a "color" announcer for the 1974 Solons, and a member of the Sacramento Athletic Hall of Fame. When interviewed for Jack Spalding's book, *Always on Sunday*, Sacramento sports editor Bill Conlin talked about Gordon as "Sacramento's best baseball player of modern times." Joe Gordon died in Sacramento on April 14, 1978.

Doug McWilliams Collection

JACK PICKART

John Hart Pickart was born in Sacramento on July 25, 1930. The 5-foot-10, 180-pound right-hander attended St. Mary's College in Moraga, Calif., and in 1950 he played semi-professional baseball in Susanville, Calif.

Pickart pitched in eight games for the 1951 Solons, posting a 3-2 record with a 3.92 ERA. In 1952, he got into 13 Solons games, going 3-6 and into 10 games with a team in Idaho Falls (Pioneer League), going 2-6. In 1953 he served in the military during the Korean conflict.

By 1954 Pickart was back with the Solons but got into only five games with a 1-1 record. His last professional baseball season was in 1955, when he appeared in only one game for the Solons, but was in 19 games (going 4-4), with the Colorado Springs Sky Sox (Western League) and in 10 games with the Modesto Reds (California League), going 3-4.

JAMES "BOZO" DEYO

James Franklin "Bozo" Deyo Jr. was born in Big Springs, Texas, on May 9, 1930.

He appeared in 24 games as an outfielder for the Solons from 1952 through 1954. He died in Sacramento on Jan. 14, 2002.

ALBERT "AL" ANICICH

Albert George Anicich was born in Sacramento on Jan. 3, 1931. The 6-foot, 185-pound right-hander was an All-City baseball player at Christian Brothers High School and went on to play for St. Mary's College in Moraga, Calif. In 1952, he played in the outfield in 63 games for the Solons.

Anicich served in the Army from 1953 through 1955 during the Korean conflict. After his professional baseball career, he worked for IBM and Buckmaster Business Machines. He married Barbara McCutcheon and they had six children: Mike, Vince, Chris, Melinda, Kerry, and Cindy.

Anicich was a coach and leader in local American Legion baseball. He was a pitching coach at Cordova High School, and a member of the LaSalle Club Hall of Fame. He died in Sacramento on Aug. 8, 2005.

ROGER "ROG" OSENBAUGH

Roger "Rog" Taber Osenbaugh was born in Sacramento on June 30, 1930. He went to McClatchy High School and played baseball, basketball and tennis. He played American Legion ball and attended Stanford University on a baseball scholarship. Osenbaugh graduated in 1952, and while there was no formal baseball draft at the time, he received six offers from major league teams. He turned them all down and accepted an offer from the Solons. He said recently in an interview that although the Solons' pay offer exceeded those from major league teams, his key reason for going with the Solons was that playing for them "had been a childhood dream."

The 6-foot-3, 180-pounder was a right-handed pitcher for the Solons from 1952 to 1953. He went into the military in July 1953, serving in the Korean conflict as a Marine Corps first lieutenant through 1954.

He returned to the Solons in the last month of the 1955 season and remained with the team through the 1959 season. He spent all seven of his professional years as a starter, finishing with a 46-66 record and a 4.19 ERA.

Osenbaugh remembers many of the players he faced, including Red Adams, Bob Alexander, Sparky Anderson, George Bamberger, Steve Bilko, Chuck Essegian, Tommy Lasorda, Gene Mauch, Willie McCovey, Earl Rapp, Brooks Robinson, Jack Salveson, Larry Sherry, Norm Sherry, Max West and Maury Wills.

He liked every one of his managers, especially Tommy Heath. He played for him in 1956 and 1957, saying, "He was an astute baseball man ... and used the personnel on the club shrewdly."

Roger Osenbaugh (Doug McWilliams Collection)

One of the managers Osenbaugh says he hated playing against was baseball icon Lefty O'Doul. In one game against the Padres, O'Doul apparently thought Osenbaugh had thrown too many "brush back" pitches, and when he came to bat, O'Doul told his pitcher to "'Knock 'im on his ass!' "

As a kid growing up in Sacramento, Osenbaugh fell in love with the Solons of the late 1930s and early '40s — especially the 1942 PCL Championship club that Pepper Martin managed and Tony Freitas led to victory. Later in his career, when pitching against the Padres in the 1950s, Osenbaugh had to face Lou Vezelich, one of his early Solons heroes, and says he was quite "staggered" by it.

After receiving his master's of business administration degree from Stanford University, Osenbaugh retired from baseball at the age of 29, and settled in Arcadia, Calif., where he stayed for 30 years. He then moved to Newport Beach, where he currently lives. In 1972, Gov. Ronald Reagan appointed him to a four-year term on the California Coastal Commission. In 1977 he formed Osenbaugh Consultants, a lobbying firm representing development interests before the Coastal Commission.

Follow Your Dream

I am struck by how Roger Osenbaugh lived his dream. He was a baseball star at Sacramento's McClatchy High School and went to Stanford on an athletic scholarship. When he graduated, Osenbaugh turned down a half-dozen lucrative offers from major league teams to play with the heroes of his youth — the Sacramento Solons. While Osenbaugh was an excellent pitcher, in the 1950's, the Solons were one of the weakest teams in the PCL, and Osenbaugh's win-loss record suffered from this lack of support.

REEVE "BUD" WATKINS

Reeve "Bud" Watkins was born in Chicago, Ill., on Jan. 23, 1931. The 6-foot-3, 205-pound right-hander attended San Mateo Junior College and the College of the Pacific (now the University of the Pacific-UOP) where he played baseball.

Watkins began his professional baseball career as a pitcher for the 1952 Stockton Ports (California League), pitching in 18 games with a 5-5 record and an ERA of 2.71. That same year he got into four games, going 1-2, for the Solons.

In 1953 he went 3-3 in 12 games for the Solons. He spent 1954 in the Army in the Korean conflict, but was back as a regular for the Solons from 1955 through 1958. During those years he started in 121 games with a 28-37 record, and a 3.25 ERA in 1957. He was a fan favorite.

Watkins split the 1959 season between two Pacific Coast League teams:

the Vancouver Mounties and the Phoenix Giants (PCL), appearing in 37 games with an 11-14 record. While he was in Phoenix, he won eight games in a row and was teammates with San Francisco Giants Hall-of-Famer Willie McCovey.

In 1960 Watkins was back with the Solons as a starter, posting a 5-3 record in 33 games. When the franchise left Sacramento to become the Honolulu Islanders, Watkins stayed with them and appeared in 41 games.

He retired from professional baseball after the 1961 season and worked in the life insurance business through 1978. That same year, he became athletic promotions director at UOP, holding that position through 1983. He then returned to the insurance business and retired in 1996. Watkins remains a very popular speaker at PCL reunions.

For the Record

Bud Watkins was a mainstay of the Solons pitching staff in the 1950s and, like Roger Osenbaugh, his win-loss record didn't reflect his great pitching ability because of the team's weakness. Watkins is a gregarious and likeable man and is a very popular "discussion panel member" at annual classic (pre-1958) Pacific Coast League player reunions.

THOMAS "TOM" AGOSTA

Thomas "Tom" Samuel Agosta was born in Sacramento on Aug. 10, 1933. He went to Sacramento High School, and was a star in football, basketball and baseball. He also attended Sacramento Junior College, now Sacramento City College. He enjoyed a seven-year professional baseball career playing primarily at second base.

Agosta was signed by the Solons in 1953, but appeared in only one game that year because he was drafted into military service.

Author's Collection

He returned to the Solons for the 1955 season, but got into only three games and was "farmed" out to the Salem Senators (Northwest League), where he was a regular in the infield playing in 129 games with a .357 batting average. He also led the league with 173 hits and 18 triples.

In 1956 Agosta appeared in 64 games for the Solons, batting .239. He also got into a total of 83 games for the two teams in the Western League, the Amarillo Gold Sox and the Albuquerque Dukes, where he hit .342.

Agosta split the 1957 season with four different ball clubs. He got into 44 games (at second base) with the New Orleans Pelicans (Southern Association), hitting .239. He also appeared at second base in 30 games for two teams in the American Association, the Indianapolis Indians and the Louisville Colonels (American Association), batting a combined .304. He also hit .287 in 45 games for the Solons, again at second base.

In 1958 Agosta split his time with three ball clubs. He got into 13 games with the Little Rock Travelers (Southern Association) and 11 games with the Louisville Colonels. He also hit .340 in 59 games with the Eugene Emeralds (Northwest League).

The next year, 1959, Agosta played in 105 games (in the outfield and at third base) for the Raleigh Capitals (Carolina League) where he hit .314 and was Carl Yazstremski's teammate. His last year of professional baseball was 1960, and he played every infield position (and in the outfield) for the Tri-City Braves (Northwest League) where he led the league batting average with a .384.

Agosta raised his family in Sacramento and retired from the Sacramento Fire Department after 28 years.

CHARLES "CHARLEY" SCHANZ

Charles "Charley" Murrell Schanz was born in Anacortes, Wash., on June 8, 1919. The 6-foot-4, 215-pound right-hander played baseball for Sacramento's Christian Brothers High School and attended Sacramento Junior College, now Sacramento City College, where he earned letters in football, basketball, baseball and tennis.

Schanz began his professional baseball career in 1938 with the Tucson Cowboys (Arizona-Texas League), where he got into 39 games with a 9-16 record and was a teammate of Bill Salkeld's. In 1939 Schanz was 10-5 with a 3.46 ERA for Tucson, earning a brief appearance (three games) with the San Francisco Seals (Pacific Coast League). He then went to the Salt Lake City Bees (Pioneer League), where he pitched in nine games with a 4-3 record.

In 1940 Schanz moved up to play for two Western International League teams — the Tacoma Tigers and the Yakima Pippins — and had an 18-9 record in 40 games. He split the 1941 season with the Salem Senators (Western International League), with a 5-4 record, and the San Francisco Seals (Pacific Coast League) where he was 0-2, with a 3.17 ERA. In 1942 he pitched in 34 games for Tacoma, going 18-13 with a 3.00 ERA, and setting a

WIL record with 29 complete games. In 1943 he became a regular with the San Diego Padres (PCL), appearing in 44 games and posting a 17-18 record and a 3.23 ERA.

The Philadelphia Phillies signed Schanz for the 1944 season, and he pitched for them through the 1947 season, posting a 28-43 record with a 4.34 ERA.

In 1948 Schanz appeared in 28 games for the Kansas City Blues (American Association), going 5 and 7, but finished the season with the Seattle Rainiers (PCL), where he was 7-6 with a 2.29 ERA. He had a great season in Seattle in 1949 with a 22-17 four-year record and a 3.25 ERA.

In an off year in the 1950 season, Schanz went 4-11 with the Seattle Rainiers, but he also spent time with the Boston Red Sox, posting a 3-2 record with them. He pitched well for Seattle during 1951 and 1952, posting a record of 14-12 over the two years and was part of the 1951 PCL Championship team.

In 1953 Schanz returned home to Sacramento and appeared in 34 games for the Solons with an 8-12 record (ERA 3.84). His final professional year in baseball was 1954, and he got into 38 games for the Solons with a 4-6 record (ERA 3.95). He was a hometown fan favorite both those years. He continued in baseball in Sacramento, managing and pitching for the semi-pro Culjis team. Among his many protégés were Buck Martinez and Larry Bowa. Schanz's son Kevin remembers his dad pitching — on occasion — until he was in his early 60s. In the 1950s, Schanz was instrumental in founding and maintaining the Land Park Pacific Little League in Sacramento. His family is still active in the league.

After his professional baseball career, Schanz worked briefly for Saccani Distributing as a warehouseman and delivery driver. After that, he spent nearly 30 years with Phillips 66 as a warehouseman and warehouse manager. He died in Sacramento on May 28, 1992.

NEILL "WILD HORSE" SHERIDAN

Neill Rawlins "Wild Horse" Sheridan was born in Sacramento on Nov. 20, 1921. The 6-foot-1, 195-pound right-hander attended Sacramento High School, and played football and ran track, but did not play baseball. Sheridan also attended the University of San Francisco where he played football, but not baseball.

Sheridan did play semi-professional baseball well enough to be signed by the San Francisco Seals (Pacific Coast League) in 1943. He appeared in one game that year. He began the 1944 season with the Chattanooga Lookouts (Southern

Doug McWilliams Collection

Association), where he played in the outfield and batted .326. His success with Chattanooga earned him a trip back to San Francisco in the latter half of 1944, when he hit .290.

Sheridan became a regular outfielder — playing both right and center for the Seals from 1945 though 1947 — and batting .283. At the end of the 1947 season, the Seals traded him to Boston, but he saw limited action with the Red Sox.

In 1948 he found himself back in the PCL, this time with the Seattle Rainiers. He batted .312 in 1948 and .259 in 1949. Seattle traded him back to the Seals in 1950, and he hit .288.

In 1951 Sheridan appeared in only 56 games with the Seals and the San Diego Padres (PCL), hitting only .204. He spent the latter half of the season with the Minneapolis Millers (American Association) and brought his average back up to .306. In 1952, Sheridan played in 34 games for the Toronto Maple Leafs and in 72 for the San Antonio Browns.

In 1953 Sheridan spent a full season in the PCL, splitting time with the Oakland Oaks and the Solons, hitting .293. Sheridan's final professional baseball season was in 1954. He appeared in 22 PCL games with the Solons and the Seals, and in 95 games with the Victoria Tyees and the Vancouver Capilanos.

All together, Sheridan played in 1,447 professional baseball games, with a lifetime batting average of .283. After baseball he went into the retail grocery business. He lives in the San Francisco Bay Area.

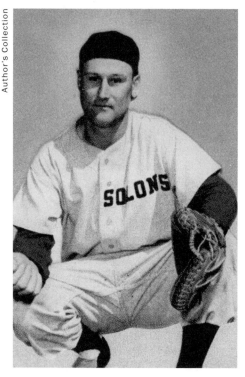

LEROY "LEE" WINTER

Leroy R. Winter was born in Orland, Calif., on Oct. 3, 1924. The 6-foot, 185-pound right-hander played baseball at Hamilton City High School in Hamilton City, Calif.

During World War II, Winter was an Army Air Corps pilot and was shot down over Foggio, Italy. He managed to escape a POW camp and find his way back to England where he encountered his brother who was being debriefed by the 8th Air Force on the same day! His brother had been shot down over France and was helped back to England by the French underground. The brothers hadn't seen each other for quite sometime, and neither one knew the other had been shot down!

Winter was signed by the Solons in 1947 and was catcher for the team's farm club, the Wenatchee Chiefs (Western International League). He was with the Grand Rapids (Mich.) Jets (Central League) for the 1948 season, but was back with the Chiefs in 1949. After that season, the Solons sold him to the Great Falls (Mont.) Selectrics (Pioneer League), where he had three good years, hitting .303 in 1952. In fact, he played so well that after the 1952 season, the Solons bought him back and he caught 16 games for them in 1953.

Winter retired from baseball after the 1953 season and spent the next 21 years with the Sacramento County Sheriff's Department. He and his family live in the Sacramento area.

THOMAS "RABBIT" GLAVIANO

Thomas Giatano "Rabbit" Glaviano was born in Sacramento on Oct. 26, 1923. The 5-foot-9, 175-pound right-hander attended Sacramento High School and played semi-pro ball in Chico in 1940. Glaviano also had a 13-year career in professional baseball as a middle infielder.

Glaviano began his career in 1941 with the Fresno Cardinals (California

League), appearing in 67 games, primarily at shortstop, and batting .253. He began the 1942 season with Fresno, getting into 67 games, but spent the second half of the season with the Springfield (Ill.) Cardinals (Middle Atlantic League), where he got into 62 games. He was in the military from 1943 through 1945.

In 1946, Glaviano was back in baseball (as a regular again), with the Fresno Cardinals (California League), where he hit .338 and led the league with 142 runs and 64 stolen bases. He was the regular third baseman in 1947 for the Houston Buffalos (Texas League), where he hit .245 in 125 games. In 1948, he was at third base for the Columbus Redbirds (American Association), hitting .287 in 106 games.

In 1949 the St. Louis Cardinals signed Glaviano as an infielder, and he spent the next five years in the major leagues. He played in 87 games that year for the Cards, primarily at third base, hitting .267. In 1950, he appeared in 115 Cards games, most often at third, and improved his hitting to .285. During the 1951 and 1952 seasons, his offense fell off, and he appeared in fewer games. In 1953 he was sold to the Philadelphia Phillies, where he appeared in just 53 games and had a .203 batting average.

In 1954 Glaviano was back in Sacramento. He appeared in 113 games for the Solons, played all four infield positions, and had a .213 average. In 1955, he was in 116 games with a .228 average. Glaviano did not play in 1956, and in 1957 had his last professional baseball season, getting into 12 games for the San Antonio Missions (Texas League).

Doug McWilliams Collection

RONALD "RONNIE" KING

Ronald "Ronnie" Anthony King was born in Sacramento on April 16, 1928. He went to Christian Brothers High School, where he played football and baseball, and graduated in 1946. The 6-foot-1, 180-pounder threw right-handed and batted left-handed. He had an eight-year career as a professional baseball player and was a coach, manager and baseball scout for four decades beyond that.

King's first affiliation with professional baseball was from 1937 through 1940 when he was the Solons' visitors' batboy. From 1940 through 1942 he ran the scoreboard at Cardinal Field, and from 1942 through 1946 he worked in the visitors' clubhouse, attending to uniforms and equipment.

He began his pro-baseball career in 1947, catching in 51 games for the Bakersfield Indians (California League). He started the 1948 season with Bakersfield, but ended up spending most of the season catching in 77 games for the Billings (Mont.) Mustangs (Pioneer League), hitting .303. In 1949 he got into 80 games for the Dayton Indians (Central League) with a .243 batting average.

King began the 1950 season with Dayton (Central League), but finished with the Cedar Rapids Indians (Three-I League), catching in 77 games. In 1951 and 1952 he served in the Army during the Korean conflict.

He was back in baseball in 1953 with the Reading Indians (Eastern League), catching in 91 games and batting .216. In 1954 he had a 30-game stay catching for the Solons in his hometown.

In 1955 he was traded to Oregon's Salem Senators (Northwest League), where he hit .250 in 59 games. He also pitched in 25 games, with a 7-1 record and a 4.24 ERA, and did some coaching, too. In 1956, his last professional season, King hit .251 in 82 games and pitched in 13 games with a 2-8 record for the Senators. He also filled in for the team manager on the road.

For the next 10 years, King worked for the local school district and began scouting for the Pittsburgh Pirates in 1961. He also scouted for the Los Angeles Dodgers from 1974 to 1988, the Philadelphia Phillies from 1988 to 1991, and again for the Pirates from 1991 though 2000.

HOLLIS "BUD" SHEELY

Hollis Kimball "Bud" Sheely was born in Spokane, Wash., on Nov. 26, 1920. He was the son of Earl Sheely, who played for the Sacramento Senators in 1928 and managed the Solons from 1944 to 1946. "Bud" played collegiate baseball at St. Mary's College in Moraga, Calif., and was elected to its Hall of Fame.

Sheely began his professional baseball career as a catcher for the 1946 Hollywood Stars (Pacific Coast League) and played with them through the 1947 season. He spent parts of the 1949 and 1950 seasons with the Oakland Oaks (PCL) and parts of the 1950 and 1951 seasons with Seattle Rainiers (PCL). He was with the Chicago White Sox from 1951 to 1953.

Sheely played for the Solons from 1954 to 1955 and retired from professional baseball after the 1955 season. He was in the PCL for seven seasons with a lifetime batting average of .248. He and his wife, Jo, owned and operated three Pancake Parade restaurants in the Sacramento area. The Sheely children are Judi, Pam and Mike. "Bud" Sheely died in Sacramento on Oct. 17, 1985.

GUS STATHOS

Gus Thomas Stathos was born in Sacramento on March 6, 1927. He graduated from McClatchy High School in 1945. During his first three years, he participated in track, football, and baseball. After his junior year, Stathos signed a contract with the Philadelphia Phillies and was not allowed to compete in high school sports during his senior year. After graduation, he served in the U.S. Navy, and at the end of World War II, he ended up on one of the Navy's baseball teams. The 6-foot-1, 180-pound right-hander enjoyed a nine-year professional baseball career as an outfielder.

After his military service, Stathos had a short stay — 16 games in 1946 — with the Phillies' farm club, the Salina (Kan.) Blue Jays (Western Association). In 1947 the Brooklyn Dodgers picked up his contract, and Stathos went to spring training with the Dodgers in Vero Beach, Fla. One of his teammates was Jackie Robinson. Stathos was farmed out to the Johnstown (Pa.) Johnnies (Middle Atlantic League), where he became a regular, hitting .311 in 108 games. The 1948 season was split between the Santa Barbara Dodgers (California League) and the Albuquerque Dukes (West Texas-New Mexico League), where Stathos hit .307 and .340, respectively.

Stathos played for the Pueblo (Colo.) Dodgers (Western League) in 1949 and 1950, with a .269 batting average over the two years. He split time

Doug McWilliams Collection

in 1951 with Santa Barbara and the Miami Sun Sox (Florida International League), where he hit .283 for manager Pepper Martin. In 1952 he played semi-professional ball for the Winnipeg (Manitoba) Giants.

In 1953 he was back in the professional game, hitting .321 in 119 games for the Calgary Stampeders (Western International League), which was managed by Gene Lilliard, a former Solon. Stathos' last year of pro baseball was 1954. He hit .306 with Calgary in 46 games and finished in 37 games for the Solons, hitting .237.

In 1955, Stathos went to spring training with the Solons, and was going to be sent to play for a team in Texas. He chose instead to go into the family bar business, which included Frank's Club, Keystone and the Arch Café bars, and that's where he stayed for the next 20 years. He dabbled in the car-wash business for a short while, but spent the next several years working for Sebastiani Wines.

JOHN "JOHNNY" BRIGGS

John "Johnny" Briggs was born in Natoma, Calif., on Jan. 24, 1934, and grew up in Folsom, where he attended Folsom High School. The 5-foot-10, 175-pound right-hander began his professional baseball career in 1952 with the Idaho Falls Russetts (Pioneer League), where he was 13-11 with an ERA of 4.4. He was with Idaho Falls again in 1953 and had a 6-6 record.

In 1954 he was 20-8 with the Salem Senators (Western International League). In 1955 he pitched for the Solons with a 15-15 record and a 3.44 ERA. In 1956 he appeared in three games with the Chicago Cubs and 18 games with the Los Angeles Angels (Pacific Coast League).

In 1957 he was in 21 games with the Fort Worth Panthers (Texas League), 14 games with the San Diego Padres (PCL) and three games with the Chicago Cubs. In 1958 he appeared in three games with Fort Worth and 20 games with the Chicago Cubs. In 1959 he appeared in four games with the Cubs and had an outstanding tour with the Padres, appearing in 24 games with a 14-6 record and a 2.60 ERA.

In 1960 Briggs was in the majors, playing in a total of 29 games for the Cleveland Indians and the Kansas City A's. In 1961, he was back in AAA ball with the Indianapolis Indians (American Association), where he got into 22 games and went 3-1 with a 2.91 ERA. His final season of professional baseball was 1962. This time pitching for the San Diego Padres, with a 4-4 record.

After his baseball career, Briggs was in the retail and real estate business in the Folsom area.

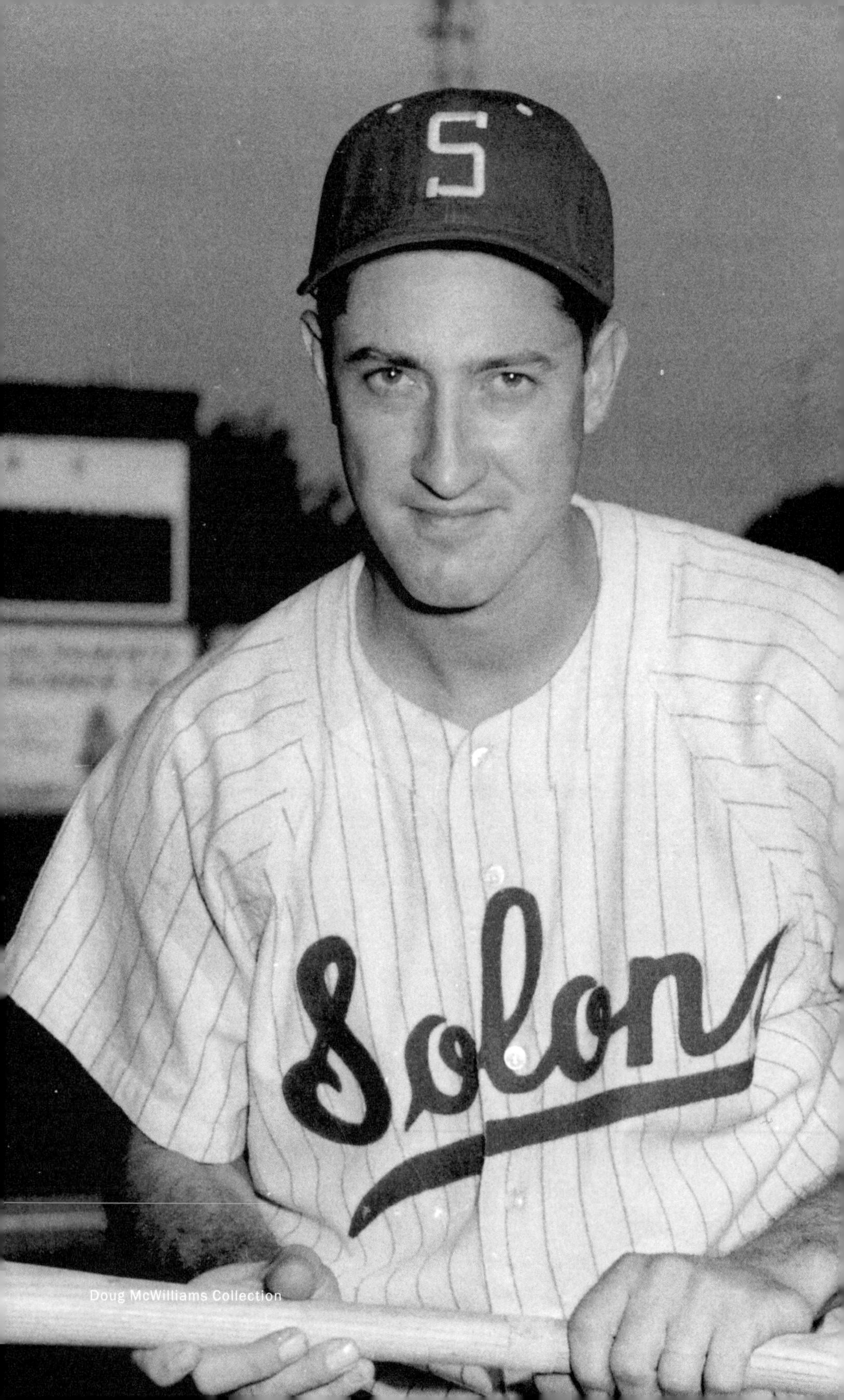

Doug McWilliams Collection

HARRY BRIGHT

Harry James Bright was born in Kansas City, Mo., on Sept. 22, 1929. The 6-foot, 190-pound right-hander played professional baseball for three years for the Solons and for eight years in the major leagues, primarily as a first baseman.

Bright began his professional career in 1946 catching in four games with the Fond du Lac Panthers (Wisconsin State League). He also appeared behind the plate in seven games for the Twin Falls Cowboys (Pioneer League). In 1947 he had short stays with the Odessa Oilers (Longhorn League), the Independence Yankees (Kansas-Oklahoma-Missouri League) and the Houma Indians (Evangeline League). Bright did not play professionally in 1948, but became a regular with the Miami (Okla.) Owls (Kansas-Oklahoma-Missouri League) in 1949, where he hit .286.

In 1950 Bright appeared in 16 games for Sioux Falls (S. D.) (Northern League), and 95 games with the Clovis Pioneers (West Texas-New Mexico League), leading the league with a .413 batting average. In 1951 he played both third and first base with the Topeka Owls (Western Association), hitting a solid .330. Bright managed the Janesville Cubs (Wisconsin State League) putting himself into 119 games at third base, in the outfield and behind the plate batting .325. In 1953 he appeared in 140 games at various positions for the Memphis Chickasaws (Southern Association), hitting .295. Bright began the 1954 season with the Buffalo Bisons (International League) and finished with the Little Rock Travelers (Southern Association), hitting .332.

Bright began 1955 with Little Rock, but got into 120 games for the Solons that year. From 1955 through 1957, Bright was with the Solons, usually playing second or third base. He played on a regular basis, appearing in 397 games with a .283 batting average.

Bright was an MLB rookie in 1958, getting into 15 games with the Pittsburgh Pirates that year. The Pirates used him sparingly during 1959 and 1960, and he was traded to the Washington Senators for the 1961 season. His best year in the majors was 1962 when he hit .273 for the Senators in 113 games.

In 1963 Bright ended up with the New York Yankees, where he was the final out in game one of the World Series against the Dodgers and was Sandy Koufax's 15th strikeout. The Yankees used him sparingly in 1964, and he went to the Chicago Cubs in 1965 where he got into 27 games, hitting .280.

After he left the Cubs, Bright managed for seven years in the Oakland A's' farm system, scouted for the Montreal Expos and managed the Solons in

1975. Greg Van Dusen, a public relations director and a radio announcer for the Solons, talked about Bright as a "colorful, Runyonesque character" with "a passion for the game and life." As a manager, Bright became known for his dislike of umpires. Once, during a game, he climbed a backstop and dropped his trousers to show his displeasure. After retiring from baseball, he settled in Sacramento. He died in Sacramento on March 13, 2000.

Craig Rader Collection

JOHN MCNAMARA

John Francis McNamara was born in Sacramento on June 4, 1932. The 5-foot-10, 175-pound right-hander attended Christian Brothers High School and Sacramento Junior College (now Sacramento City College).

McNamara had an 18-year professional baseball career as a catcher, all in the minor leagues. He began his career in 1951 with the Fresno Cardinals (California League). In 1952 he appeared briefly with the Houston Buffalos (Texas League) and caught most of the season with the Lynchburg Cardinals (Piedmont League).

From 1953 though 1954, McNamara served in the military during the Korean conflict. In 1955 he returned to baseball, this time catching for the Lewiston Broncs (Northwest League).

In 1956 he appeared in 76 games for the Solons and 29 games for the Albuquerque Dukes (Western League). In 1957 he split time between the Tulsa Oilers (Texas League) and the Amarillo Gold Sox (Western League).

From 1958 though 1962 McNamara was a regular with the Lewiston Broncs (Northwest League) where he hit .259. He started his managerial career with Lewiston, managing the club from 1959 through 1962.

McNamara managed the Binghamton Triplets (Eastern League) in 1963, putting himself into 69 games. In 1964, he managed the Dallas Rangers (Pacific Coast League) appearing in 13 games as a player. In 1965 he managed the Birmingham Barons (Southern League), and in 1966 the Mobile A's (also in the Southern League). In 1967 he was back managing Birmingham.

McNamara had a 20-year career in the major leagues, managing six teams through 2,395 games (.485). From 1969 to 1970, he managed the Oakland A's; from 1974 to 1977, the San Diego Padres; from 1979 to 1982, the Cincinnati Reds; from 1983 to 1984, the California Angels; from 1985 to 1988, the Boston Red Sox; from 1990 to 1991, the Cleveland Indians; and, in 1996, he managed the California Angels. The highlight of his career came in 1986 when the Red Sox won the American League pennant, and he was named American League manager of the year.

WALDON "WALLY" WESTLAKE

Waldon "Wally" Thomas Westlake was born in Gridley, Calif., on Nov. 8, 1920. Westlake grew up in Sacramento and played baseball for Christian Brothers High School.

The 185-pound, 6-foot-1 right-hander played professional baseball for 14 years, beginning in 1940. After the 1939 Sacramento Winter League season (a local semi-professional league), "Wally" was signed as an outfielder by the Brooklyn Dodgers' organization. In the spring of 1940, he went to spring training with the Class A Elmira Pioneers ball club, with a contract paying $125 per month. Before the season began, he was sent down to the Dayton Wings (Mid-Atlantic League). He played there professionally for the first time. His contract had a clause stating that if he was still with the Dodgers' organization as of June 15, 1940, he would get a $500 bonus. He said for that amount of money, he could buy a new Ford. Unfortunately, he was not performing well, and on June 14, he was handed a Greyhound bus ticket back to Sacramento. To make matters worse, when the bus left town that night it went right past the lighted ball field where the game was in progress. Westlake was devastated and sure that his baseball career was over at the ripe old age of 19.

The Beast
Wally was affectionately called "the beast" by his Pirates teammates because of his tough demeanor. He had such an outstanding rookie season in 1947 that he earned the runner up position to Jackie Robinson as Rookie of the Year.

But he was back in the game in 1941 as a regular outfielder with the Merced Bears (California League), and his game improved. In 1942 he moved up as starting outfielder for the Oakland Oaks (Pacific Coast League), and he appeared in 169 games, primarily as a right fielder. He said that he was both thrilled and somewhat intimidated that season when he had to hit against one of his Solons heroes, PCL Hall-of-Famer Tony Freitas.

During World War II, Westlake joined the U.S. Coast Guard, and served from 1943 through 1945. He thought he was going off to war, but word about his prowess as a ballplayer preceded him and he was asked to join the

Wally Westlake Collection

Coast Guard's baseball team. He never left the West Coast, and became what he termed a "Broadway Commando." He did get to see some of his friends who played for other services branches, such as Joe Marty who was in the Army, when the teams played each other.

After the war in 1946, Westlake took up where he left off in the Oakland outfield, hitting a solid .315. His game improved that season when Casey Stengel, the Oaks' manager, took him under his wing and taught him how to be a "thinking" ballplayer. He remembers Stengel telling him there was "more to playing baseball than catching the ball and throwing it back to the infield."

Westlake's outstanding 1946 season moved him up to the Pittsburgh Pirates in 1947. That began a 10-year major league career. For the next four years he was a Pirates regular. His Pirates roommates and good friends included Ernie

"Tiny" Bonham and later, future Hall-of-Famer Ralph Kiner. He felt some satisfaction with his success in Pittsburgh after his not-so-great experience with the Dodgers organization in Dayton, when the Dodgers tried to trade for him. He was disappointed when the trade did not go through because as he said recently, "Ebbets Field was a great place to swing a bat," and his batting average and career would have benefited.

In 1951 he spent part of the season with the Pirates and part with the St. Louis Cardinals. He was an All-Star that year. One of the players coming from the Cards in the 1951 trade was Joe Garagiola, who later became a well-known announcer. In 1952 Westlake appeared with the Cards, the Cincinnati Reds and later the Cleveland Indians.

Westlake spent the next four seasons with the Indians, which included playing in the 1954 World Series with Hall-of-Fame pitcher Bob Lemon (who would manage the Solons in 1974). His roommate and lifelong good friend was third baseman Al Rosen. Even though he felt that Al Lopez, the Indians' manager, was one of the best ever in baseball, Westlake left the Indians during the 1955 season, and spent time with the Baltimore Orioles, and the Pacific Coast League teams, the Oakland Oaks and the Portland Beavers. He had a lifetime MLB batting average of .272.

In 1956 "Wally" appeared in five games for the Philadelphia Phillies, returned home to Sacramento and was in 90 games for the Solons. His PCL lifetime batting average was .280.

After his baseball career, Westlake worked for and retired from Teichert Construction. He and his wife, Rose, had five children: Patricia, Constance, Wally Jr., Kathleen and Joe. Westlake said recently that through baseball he "met some fine people," and made lifelong friendships. He is a member of the Sacramento Athletic Hall of Fame.

"CUNO" BARRAGAN

Facundo Antonio "Cuno" Barragan was born in Sacramento on June 20,1932. He grew up around 13th and Q streets and began playing "street ball" (baseball) when he was about 5. Sometimes he and his friends played "hardball" on the softball field at 10th and P streets. Barragan started playing organized baseball in the old Sacramento summer recreation league in the 100-pound division when he was about 10. He remembers that the league was very competitive yet enjoyable. Barragan became the second-string catcher on the Sutter Junior High School team, and the year before he graduated, he

was the second-string catcher on the 1949 state champion Sacramento High School team. At Sacramento Junior College, now Sacramento City College, he was the fourth-string catcher. Discouraged, he quit after his first year and went to work laying tile. In the fall of 1951, Barragan was talked into joining the SJC football team where he was a 5-foot-11, 165-pound offensive guard and linebacker and earned "most valuable player" honors. That success encouraged him to go back to baseball in the spring. He became the first-string catcher and led the team with a .408 batting average.

Barragan also played on a couple of other local amateur teams, was scouted by several professional baseball clubs, and in 1952 signed with the Solons. He had a great time at spring training in Santa Cruz, where he met several famous players including "Nippy" Jones, Jess Flores and Al Heist. He spent the 1953 season with the Idaho Falls Russetts (Pioneer League).

In 1954 and 1955 Barragan served in the U.S. Navy. In 1956 he again went to spring training with the Solons, but ended up with the Amarillo (Texas) Gold Sox (Western League) managed by former Hollywood star Chuck Stevens. That season he had 10 home runs and was moved up to the Solons in 1957. Barragan played in more than 100 games for the Solons, although 1957 was not a very good baseball year (his batting average was .197), due in part to injuries and hometown pressure. His manager, Tommy Heath, was considered one of the best in the PCL, and Barragan enjoyed playing under his leadership.

In 1958 the Solons attempted to send Barragan to the Double-A, Atlanta (Ga.) Crackers (affiliated with the Milwaukee Braves) for more "seasoning." At that point, he felt that he had enough "seasoning," refused to go, was suspended from baseball, and returned to laying tile in Sacramento at the Fischer Tile Company.

Heath, who had managed Barragan and the Solons in 1957, was by 1958 manager of the Portland Beavers (PCL). In June, Heath and the Beavers were in town to play the Solons. Both of Portland's catchers were injured and Heath asked about Barragan. Since the Solons had three catchers at that time, they were willing to let him go, but, because of league rules, needed to receive some compensation, so Sacramento was paid $1 for his services. Barragan played for the Beavers for two weeks before returning to the tile business.

In 1959 Bill Brenner, the Solons' general manager, asked Barragan to spring training, and Barragan came to the attention of Bobby Bragan, manager of the Dodgers' top farm team, the Spokane Indians (Northwestern League).

Bragan made a deal for Barragan's services for the year — again $1 to the Solons. Barragan enjoyed the season, sharing catching duties with Norm Sherry and playing with the likes of Frank Howard, Steve Bilko and Chuck Essegian. At the end of the season, he returned to Sacramento.

In 1960, Barragan shared catching duties with Bob Roselli, hitting .318 and throwing out 24 runners attempting to steal. "I was a good receiver and I could throw," he said in an interview. The Chicago Cubs selected him in the minor league draft that year, and he had a strong showing in spring training in 1961. The job of starting catcher was nearly his, but in March he broke his ankle during an exhibition game against Cleveland (he hit a double off Jim Perry), and he missed all except the final month of the 1961 season. His first game as a Cub was Sept. 1, 1961, when he played against the San Francisco Giants at Wrigley Field. He sent left-hander Dick LeMay's fastball over the left-field wall for a line-drive home run.

In 1962 Barragan was a part-time player, hitting just .201, but he continued to show strong defense. He shared catching duties with Dick Bertell and Mo Thacker. Barragan was one of the few catchers to throw out Maury Wills, who at the time was in the process of setting a season record of 104 steals. On May 16, he injured his right hand when it was hit by a foul tip.

In 1963 Barragan got up to bat only once because the Cubs had acquired three younger catchers in trade. He spent most of the season with the Salt Lake City Cubs, where he hit .285. His last professional baseball game was the Hispanic All-Star Game on Oct. 12, 1963. It also was the final game played at New York's Polo Grounds. Barragan was catcher for all nine innings, and his National League team won 5-2. He fondly remembers catching Juan Marichal and being in the company of Marichal, Orlando Cepeda, Felipe Alou and Roberto Clemente.

It was during Barragan's Cub years that Wrigley used a "college of coaches" rather than one decision-making manager. The results, both in winning and morale, were not good. "It was the worst three years to have been a Cub," Barragan said in an interview.

After the season Barragan was traded to the Los Angeles Dodgers who wanted him to work the 1964 season with the young pitchers at their Spokane

Cuno

When I was first introduced to Barragan a few years ago, I found him likable and fun to talk to. I also found a great story about a "kid" from Sacramento who overcame his challenges and went on to play nine years of professional baseball.

affiliate. Barragan was 31 and had a family to support, so rather than taking a $4,000 pay cut, he retired from professional baseball.

He wanted to find a high school teaching job that came with a baseball coaching position, but he ultimately went into the insurance business with CalWestern Life and created a successful career.

Barragan remembers Edmonds Field as an excellent ballpark that was well maintained and liked by visiting ball clubs. Neither the heat of Sacramento summers, nor the wool uniforms ever bothered him. The best thing about playing for the Solons, he says, was that it was a hometown crowd and he could live in Sacramento.

In 1973, Barragan was inducted into the Mexican-American Sports Association Hall of Fame, and in 2002, the La Salle Club Hall of Fame and the Sacramento City College Athletic Hall of Fame. He is married and has three grown sons: Michael, Steve and David.

Barragan says one of his greatest thrills was the opportunity to work hard and get to the big leagues at a time when there were only eight teams in the National League. He remembers playing against many of the greats: Hank Aaron, Stan Musial, Don Drysdale, Warren Spahn, Bob Gibson, Sandy Koufax and Willie Mays. His inner strength, he says, carried him a long way. "That's my story and I'm going to stick to it!"

Doug McWilliams Collection

JAMES "JIM" WESTLAKE

James "Jim" Patrick Westlake was born in Sacramento on July 3, 1930. He played baseball at McClatchy High and graduated in 1948. The 6-foot, 190-pound left-hander played professionally — at first base and in the outfield — for 10 seasons. In 1948, he played in 79 games for the Salt Lake City Bees (Pioneer League), and 1949, 113 games. His batting average over the two years was .323.

In 1949 he was in 40 games with the San Francisco Seals (Pacific Coast League). In 1950 he got into

13 games with the Seals and 151 games with the Yakima Bears (Northwest League). Westlake also toured Japan with Lefty O'Doul.

During the Korean conflict, Westlake served in the U.S. Coast Guard (from 1951 through 1953). He was stationed in Hawaii.

In 1954 he returned to professional baseball, and was the regular first baseman for the San Francisco Seals, hitting .285 in a 142 games. He spent the 1955 season with the AAA Syracuse club where he hit .262 in 144 games, and he also played briefly with the Philadelphia Phillies that year. In 1956 he played with the Vancouver Mounties (Pacific Coast League) hitting .246 in 125 games.

In 1957 he returned home to Sacramento with the Solons, played first base and in the outfield, and batted .285. In 1958 he played 130 games for the Solons, hitting .266.

Westlake finished his professional career in 1959, appearing in 110 games for the Portland Beavers (PCL) and hitting .246. His six-year PCL batting average was .266.

After baseball, Westlake had a distinguished 40-plus year career as a representative for Scott-Naake Paper Company. He and his wife, Alba, had four children: Thomas, Elaine, Scott and Sandra. He died in Sacramento on Jan. 3, 2003.

WILLIAM "BILL" MCNULTY

William Francis McNulty was born in Sacramento on Aug. 29, 1946. He played Little League baseball in Roseville and later attended Highlands High School, where he was a standout player in football, basketball and baseball, and graduated in 1964. McNulty had an 11-year professional baseball career, primarily as a third baseman.

Bill's father, Ray McNulty, played professional baseball in the Pacific Coast League as a pitcher for the Portland Beavers and San Francisco Seals in the late 1940s and early 1950s.

Baseball scout Don Pries brought John McNamara, a Sacramento native and manager of the AA Modesto A's, to visit McNulty and encourage him to become part of the Kansas City A's organization. McNulty signed as an amateur free agent for the A's in 1965.

McNulty began playing professionally in 1965 with the Leesburg A's (Florida State League), where he was a teammate of the A's Hall-of-Famer Rollie Fingers. In 1966 he was a regular with the Burlington (Iowa) Bees

(Midwest League), where he hit .259. Later that season he appeared briefly, hitting .409 in seven games, for the Mobile (Ala.) A's (Southern League).

In 1967, McNulty split time between the Birmingham (Ala.) A's (Southern League) and the Peninsula Grays (Carolina League), with a combined .250 batting average. In 1968 McNulty split the season again, playing 48 games for the Birmingham A's and 54 games for the Grays, where he hit .290.

In 1969 he hit .288 in 75 games for the Birmingham A's, got into five games with the Oakland A's, and finished the season playing in 26 games with the Iowa Oaks (American Association).

McNulty was a regular with the Oaks in 1970 and 1971, getting into 106 games, hitting .295; and 107 games, hitting .247. In 1971, he led the league in home runs with 27.

In 1972 McNulty played four games at third base for the Oakland A's; however, his contract was then sold to the Milwaukee Brewers organization. That year he set a league record for 137 games for the Brewers' farm club, the Evansville Triplets (American Association).

He spent the 1973 season in the infield for the Tidewater Tides (International League), playing in 140 games, hitting .248 and leading the league in doubles.

In 1974 McNulty played third base for the Solons and hit .329. He topped the Pacific Coast League in five categories: (1) games played: all 144 of them! (2) total bases: 363 (3) runs scored: 135 (4) runs batted in: 135 and (5) home runs: 55. For his achievements he was named to the PCL All-Star team and was the Solons Most Valuable Player. At 6-foot-4 and 205 pounds, McNulty was a big man. No wonder Jim Jenkins, a *Sacramento Union* sportswriter, called him the "Sacramento strongman."

In 1975 McNulty played 40 games for the Solons with a .305 batting average. Later in 1975 he played for Lotte in the Japanese League and retired when the season ended. When reflecting on his experience in Japanese baseball, he said, "It was easy to see that Japanese baseball stars could play at our major league level."

Because he had a long minor-league career and hit more than 200 minor-league home runs (something he considered "a dubious honor"), McNulty

said he could be likened to Crash Davis, the character in the movie *Bull Durham*. He remembers that when he played, "the minimum big-league pay was $15,000 and that seemed like a lot back then." He also remembers "low-ball pitchers and highball drinkers, but no one was taking game-enhancing drugs."

McNulty moved to the Seattle area where he and his wife, Susan, raised their daughter, Heidi. He is a sales manager for a power tool company and enjoys golf and fishing.

"Baseball transcends time," McNulty says. "It is our link to history and it is a place where families can go and share the spirit of ancient heroes and the competitive lessons of team work. Baseball is as much a part of our heritage in Sacramento as the Gold Rush. I'm glad they built a great park in Sacramento. The fans deserve a quality gathering place to celebrate a game that has meant so much for the past 125 years."

Solons team-signed balls, 1950's (Author's Collection)

1939 pitcher's warm-up jacket (Author's Collection)

OTHER PLAYERS AND PERSONS OF NOTE

*A*uthor's note: I started out to do a book strictly about Sacramentans who played for Sacramento, but along the way found players, coaches, pitchers, club owners and hall-of-famers who earned a place in Sacramento's baseball history. They were famous — or infamous — and contributed in some way to our professional baseball legacy.

SAMCC

CHARLES "TRUCK" EAGAN

Charles Eugene "Truck" Eagan was born in San Francisco on Aug. 10, 1877. He played shortstop with a .276 batting average in the California League from 1899 through 1902, the last three years with Sacramento, including with the Gilt Edge league champions in 1900. He played briefly in the major leagues with the Pittsburgh Pirates and Cleveland Blues in 1901. Eagan played in the Pacific Coast League for another seven years, including a stint with the Sacramento Senators in 1903 and with the PCL's champion Tacoma Tigers in 1904, when he hit .311. Eagan was the regular shortstop for the Tigers in 1905 and for the Fresno Raisin Eaters (Pacific Coast League) in 1906. In 1907 and 1908, he played for the Oakland Oaks and in 1909 for the Vernon Tigers.

In 1900, a Gilt Edge program said: "The first game where 'Truckerino' Eagan fails to make a home run will make the heart of the small boy sad. It has come to be expected that 'Eagan' will put the ball over the fence in his favorite locality during each game — and has been occasioning no disappointment recently."

Eagan appeared in 1,362 PCL games with a lifetime PCL batting average of .286. He led the league in home runs in 1904 with 24 and again in 1905 with 21. He was inducted into the PCL Hall of Fame in 2003. Carlos Bauer, author of *The Pacific Coast League Cyclopedia*, recently called Eagan "the first big star of the Pacific Coast League because of his prodigious power. In 1903, Eagan blasted a league-leading 13 homers — a huge number for the dead-ball era — 23 triples, hit for .322 batting average and stole 50 bases." Charles Eagan died in San Francisco on March 3, 1949.

GRAHAM, Capt., Sacramento

Author's Collection

CHARLIE GRAHAM

Charles "Charlie" Henry Graham was born in Santa Clara, Calif., on April 25, 1878. He was associated with baseball in California for most of his life. In the late 1890s, he played baseball and coached for Santa Clara University (where there is a dormitory named in his honor) and he was the first from Santa Clara to play in the majors.

The 5-foot-11, 180-pound right-hander caught for the Sacramento Senators in the "outlaw" California League in 1902. He played for five years in the Pacific Coast League, primarily as a catcher. His PCL career began in its inaugural year, 1903, with the Sacramento Senators. He appeared in 178 games with a .268 batting average. When the team moved to Tacoma, Wash., he moved with them, playing in 149 games for the 1904 PCL champion Tigers and in

158 games for the 1905 Tigers.

Graham appeared in 30 games with the Boston Red Sox in 1906, but returned to California after the Earthquake of 1906 to help his family. Later in 1906, and again in 1907, Graham was a catcher with the Sacramento Senators.

In addition to catching in 1908, Graham managed the Senators. In 1909 he negotiated the transfer of the team from the California State League back into the Pacific Coast League. In 1910, his last PCL year as a player, he appeared in only seven games. Graham was co-owner of the Senators from 1909 through 1913 and again in 1918.

In 1919 Graham became one of three owners of the San Francisco Seals (PCL) and by the 1930s he was sole owner. (Graham's son, Charles J. Graham, was co-owner of the Solons from 1951 to 1957.) In 1931 Graham built Seals Stadium, which replaced Recreation Park. He signed Joe DiMaggio after the 1932 season, and then sold him to the New York Yankees in 1934 on the condition that DiMaggio play the 1935 season with the Seals. Graham, who is a member of the PCL Hall of Fame, ran the team until he died in San Francisco on Aug. 29, 1948.

Mark Macrae Collection

HARRY HOOPER

Harry Bartholomew Hooper was born on Aug. 24, 1887, in Bell Station, Calif. The 5-foot-10, 170-pounder threw right and batted left. He attended St. Mary's College in Oakland, Calif., studying civil engineering and playing baseball, and found employment with the Western Pacific Railroad in Sacramento. He played baseball for the Sacramento Senators ("outlaw" California State League) from 1907 through the 1908 season and made more money in baseball than he did as a civil engineer!

Hooper's outstanding baseball skills drew the notice of Boston Red Sox owner John I. Taylor during a visit to Northern California. Hooper had a beer with Taylor at a bar at Eighth and J streets and agreed to report to Red Sox spring training for a salary of $2,800. He played in right field for the Sox from 1909 to 1920. From 1910 through 1915, he was a member of one of the most outstanding outfields ever, the fabled "Million Dollar Outfield," with Tris Speaker and fellow St. Mary's graduate, Duffy Lewis. Hooper was a skilled leadoff hitter and defensive outfielder and played on four World Series Champion Red Sox teams: 1912, 1915, 1916 and 1918.

Over But Out Hooper's obituary, which has been reproduced from the original newspaper clipping at deadballera.com, talks about his crucial play in the deciding eighth game of the 1912 World Series against the New York Giants. It notes that when Hooper made a "running barehanded catch," he also fell over the fence.

Hooper also was the first to hit two home runs in a single World Series game on Oct. 13, 1915. With 300 stolen bases, Hooper remains the all-time Red Sox leader.

When Sox owner Harry Frazee sold off his best players in the late teens (including Babe Ruth), Hooper was disgusted and forced his own sale to the Chicago White Sox, playing with them from 1921 to 1925. Owner Charles Comisky hoped that a big-name player like Hooper would restore credibility to his franchise after the 1919 "Black Sox" scandal.

In 1927, Hooper played in the outfield for the San Francisco Missions (Pacific Coast League), batted .284 and also managed the Missions for most of the 1927 season. When he was through playing baseball, he worked at real estate for a while, coached baseball at Princeton University and for various California minor league clubs, and eventually became the postmaster of Capitola, Calif.

Hooper was inducted into the Baseball Hall of Fame in 1971 for his overall great play as "a steady leadoff hitter and spectacular defensive outfielder." He had a lifetime batting average of .281 and a fielding percentage of .966.

While he was captain of the Boston Red Sox in 1919, Hooper changed the course of baseball history. He convinced manager Ed Barrow to move pitcher Babe Ruth into the outfield to take greater advantage of Ruth's skills with the bat.

Hooper died in Santa Cruz, Calif., on Dec. 18, 1974.

CHARLES "SPIDER" BAUM

Charles "Spider," "Soup Bone," "Honk" Adrian Baum was born in San Francisco on May 28,1882. He won 267 games, with 52 shutouts, as a right-handed pitcher in a 15-year Pacific Coast League career between 1903 and

1920. "Spider" appeared in 630 PCL games and pitched a record 4,443 innings.

His nickname came from his frame: at 6-foot-1, he weighed a mere 165 pounds. He began his professional baseball career in 1902 with the San Francisco Ponies (California League).

When the PCL began in 1903, Baum pitched for the champion Los Angeles LooLoos, remaining with them through the 1905 season. In 1906 and 1907, he pitched for the Altoona (Pa.) Mountaineers (Tri-States League). In 1908 he managed and pitched for the Fresno Raisin Growers ("outlaw" California State League). Baum played for the Sacramento Senators from 1909 through 1912.

During the 1912 season he was sent to the Vernon Tigers (Pacific Coast League), and in 1913 was with the PCL's Venice Tigers. His best years were 1914 through 1918 when he was with the San Francisco Seals (PCL) and compiled a 103-66 record. Baum was traded to the Salt Lake City Bees (Pioneer League) in 1920, when he closed out his career.

Even when his playing days were over, "Spider" stayed in baseball for many years in the front offices of the San Francisco Seals, the Salt Lake City Bees and the San Diego Padres. Allen T. Baum, his brother, was PCL president from 1912 through 1919. Baum is a member of the PCL Hall of Fame. He died in Renton, Wash., on June 28, 1955.

GANDIL, Sacramento

Author's Collection

"CHICK" GANDIL

Charles Arnold "Chick" Gandil was born in Saint Paul, Minn., on Jan. 19, 1887. The 6-foot-2, 190-pound right-hander played in the Pacific Coast League for three years and in the major leagues for nine seasons. In 1906 he was with the Los Angeles Angels (PCL), and in 1907 with the Portland Beavers (PCL).

In 1909 he played first base for the Sacramento Senators with a .280 batting average. He was considered a "rough" individual in Sacramento, perhaps because before he could play ball, he had to be bailed out of jail. Charges of misappropriation had been brought against him by the club he had just left, the Fresno Raisin Growers of the outlaw California State League.

"Chick" moved up to the major leagues in 1910 with the Chicago White Sox. In 1911 he played for Montreal Royals (International League), from 1912 through 1915 with the Washington Senators, and in 1916 he was with the Cleveland Indians.

In 1917 the White Sox won the 1917 World Series over the New York Giants, but two years later "Chick" was the ringleader of the notorious Chicago "Black Sox" team that threw the 1919 World Series. He had a lifetime MLB batting average of .277 and a fielding percentage of .992. He later worked as a plumber in Calistoga, Calif., where he died on Dec. 13, 1970.

Mark Macrae Collection

"LEFTY" WILLIAMS

Claude Preston "Lefty" Williams was born in Aurora, Mo., on March 9, 1893. After playing in only six games with the Detroit Tigers in the 1913 and 1914 seasons, he joined the Sacramento Senators in 1914. Williams appeared in 101 PCL games in 1914 and 1915 with Sacramento, the San Francisco Missions and the Salt Lake City Bees, with a 46-32 record.

From 1916 to 1920, he pitched for the Chicago White Sox, posting an 81-44 record with a lifetime ERA of 3.13. In 1917 he went 17-8 while he was a member of what would be Chicago's last World Series championship team until 2005.

Williams, however, is best known for his involvement in the 1919 World Series "Black Sox." He issued a high number of walks and "crossed up" his catcher by not throwing the expected pitches. His record during the series was 0-3 with an ERA of 6.61! Williams died in Laguna Beach, Calif. on Nov. 4, 1959.

CLARENCE "DAZZY" VANCE

Clarence Arthur "Dazzy" Vance was born in Orient, Iowa, on March 4, 1891. The 6-foot-2, 200-pound right-hander had a 16-year major league career that culminated in his election to the Hall of Fame in 1955. According to ballparkguys.com, "Dazzy" got his colorful nickname as a child. A cowboy

ZEE-NUT
SERIES
1919
VANCE
SACTO.

he knew always asked, "Ain't that a daisy?" when he saw something he liked. When Vance tried to imitate him, however, he mispronounced daisy as "dazzy," and the nickname stuck.

Vance began his major league career in 1915 when he appeared in one game for the Pittsburgh Pirates and eight games for the New York Yankees. He was out of major league baseball in 1916 and 1917 because an injured elbow became inflamed and took several years to heal. In spite of pain from the injury, Vance was back with the Yankees in 1918.

Known for his blazing fastball, "Dazzy" pitched in 48 games for the Sacramento Senators in 1919, going 10-18 with a 2.82 ERA. Because of arm problems, he was out of major league baseball in 1920 and 1921 and was again playing in the minors, including for a team in New Orleans.

From 1922 through 1932, Vance pitched for the Brooklyn Dodgers. He led the National League in wins for two years, in ERAs for three years, in strikeouts for eight years, and was the league MVP in 1924. After spending 1933 and parts of 1934 with the St. Louis Cardinals (appearing in one game of the 1934 World Series won by the Cards) and the Cincinnati Reds, he finished his career in 1935 with the Boston Braves. His 197-140 lifetime MLB record would have been better had he played with better offensive teams. "Dazzy" Vance died in Homosassa, Fla., on Feb. 16, 1961.

FREDERICK "FRED" PEARL

Frederick Albert Pearl was born in Sacramento on Feb. 25, 1879. His family had come around the horn from England (via a stay in Australia), to work for the railroads in the 1870s.

CALIFORNIA
STATE FAIR

SACRAMENTO
Sept. 4 to 9, 1933

Pearl attended local schools including the Mary J. Watson grammar school at 16th and J streets (now the site of the Memorial Auditorium). He later attended the Howe Academy in the Pythian Castle at Ninth and I streets, where he excelled in dancing. He went on to become a dance instructor and was the assistant dance master at Turner Hall, which was over a theater on K Street between Ninth and 10th streets.

As a young man, Pearl was an enthusiastic cyclist and a very active member of the Capitol City Wheelmen bicycle club, a prominent sports and social organization. The group often would enjoy a Sunday by riding their bicycles to Auburn, playing a game of baseball against a local club there, having dinner, and then riding home again.

Pearl pursued his education at Sacramento's Atkinson Business College and later followed in his father's footsteps working as a machinist for the Southern Pacific Railroad.

Doug Dahl Collection

In the summer of 1906, Pearl set speed records with his conventional big-wheel bike, which in those days was called an "ordinary." He held the fastest time, reported to be 44 minutes, for the 15-mile stretch over dirt roads between Sacramento and Elk Grove. In the 1920s and '30s, Pearl was known for riding his high-wheeled bike in community events. In fact, Gov. Jimmy Rolph commissioned him to promote the 1933 State Fair by riding his "ordinary" throughout the state.

In addition to cycling, Pearl also was a member of the Sacramento Athletic Club, participating in their track meets and baseball games. He regularly played baseball (usually in center field) for many local recreation teams, including the Wheelmen and Elk Grove. He was later with the famous Brooke Realty team when they won the Northern California semi-pro championship and played exhibition games against PCL teams, including the Sacramento Senators.

In the early 1920s, Lew Moreing hired Pearl, who was also known for his booming voice, to be the announcer for the Sacramento Senators. In those days, baseball parks did not have public address systems, and before the game, the announcer, with a large megaphone in hand, walked from home plate up and down to first and third bases, announcing the lineups, and between innings gave scoring updates and lineup changes. Later, in the early 1930s, a public address system eliminated his job.

During his announcing days, Pearl also worked in Ancil Hoffman's cigar store at 708 K St. and expanded his athletic interests into boxing as a promoter, starting at the old L Street Arena. Max Baer, Buddy Baer, Jim Braddock (the "Cinderella Man"), and Archie Moore were among the fighters Pearl brought to Sacramento. He and legendary boxing promoter Hoffman, who was Max Baer's manager, often worked together and were lifelong friends. Pearl continued as a boxing manager and promoter through the 1960s and in 1982 was posthumously inducted into the Sacramento Valley Boxing Association Hall of Fame.

Through his announcing, boxing promotion and "ordinary"-bicycle riding, Pearl became a popular and legendary figure in Sacramento. He hunted and fished with his close friend, "Buddy" Ryan, the Senators' manager, and was a very active member of the Masons.

Pearl married Bella Shaw in 1912 and the couple had two daughters, Elizabeth and Ralpha. Ralpha married local boxer and movie actor Buddy Baer, brother of the former world heavyweight champion Max Baer. Later, she married the son of the Senators' team doctor, Dr. Roger Daniels. Pearl's last ride on his "ordinary" was in 1968 at the age of 89. He died in Sacramento on Nov. 4, 1970.

Author's Collection

GEORGE "JACK" DOWNEY

George B. "Jack" Downey was the trainer for the Sacramento Senators and Solons from the early 1920s through 1948. He and his wife, Anna, lived in midtown Sacramento within walking distance of the ball field at Riverside Boulevard and Broadway.

Downey had been a heavyweight fighter in the 1910s and even defeated Jack Dempsey in 1915. In his book *Sacramento Senators and Solons,* John Spalding recounts a fight between Downey and pitcher "Sea Lion" Hall on a train trip back to Sacramento from Salt Lake

City. Apparently, "Seal Lion" taunted Downey about his boxing skills until Downey soundly beat him in a fistfight. Much to Downey's relief, Senators' owner Lew Moreing gave Downey permission to keep Hall in line.

Author's Collection

"RAY" FRENCH

Raymond Edward "Ray" French was born in Alameda, Calif., on Jan. 9, 1895. The 5-foot-9, 160-pound right-hander had a 28-year professional baseball career, primarily as a shortstop, beginning in 1914 with the Baker City (Ore.) Miners (Western Tri-State League) where he got into 85 games and hit .339.

In 1915, French had a brief appearance (only three games) with the PCL Portland Beavers, but he became a regular at second and third bases with the Cedar Rapids Rabbits (Central Association) getting into 125 games in 1916 and 89 games in 1917. In 1918 he played third base in five games for the Vancouver Beavers (Pacific Coast International League). In 1919 French got into 88 games for the PCL Seattle Indians, hitting .221, and in 1920 he had "a cup of coffee" (got into only two games) with the New York Yankees.

In 1921 and 1922 French was a regular with the Vernon Tigers (PCL) getting into 163 and 200 games, and hitting .269 and .269, respectively. He got off to a fast start with the Tigers in 1923, hitting .307, and finished the season with the Brooklyn Dodgers, getting into 43 games and hitting .219. He was traded to the Chicago White Sox for the 1924 season, but he was used sparingly. Later that season he played shortstop for the Minneapolis Millers (American Association) hitting .246 in 67 games.

In 1925, French took over the shortstop position for the Sacramento Senators and did not relinquish it until the 1934 season. During those nine years, he was considered one of the finest shortstops in the PCL and, perhaps, Sacramento's finest of all time.

In 1934 French got into a few games for the Senators before he was traded to the Oakland Oaks, where he ended his PCL career near his hometown of Alameda. In his PCL career, he appeared in 2,159 games with 2,191 hits, had a lifetime batting average of .269 and was inducted into the PCL Hall of Fame.

In 1935 French played shortstop in 151 games for the Kansas City Blues (American Association), hitting .259. He spent the 1936 season with the Blues, but his playing time diminished to 67 games in spite of a reasonable .284 batting average. "Ray" started the 1937 season with the Blues, but was traded to the Louisville Colonels (American Association). His combined batting average that year was .256. In 1938 he got into 74 games for the Colonels, but his hitting began to taper off and that was his last year with them.

French began his managerial career in 1939 as player-manager for the Mansfield Braves (Ohio State League). He also hit .245 in 29 games as a middle infielder. Later that year he became the player-manager of the Ashland (Ky.) Colonels (Mountain State League), putting himself into 89 games (at shortstop and third base) and hitting .358. French hit .272 in 71 games at shortstop and third base in 1940. His last year as a player was 1941 when he put himself into one game at shortstop and had one at bat.

French umpired in the PCL for 10 years. Jack Clark, a writer for the *Alameda Times Star*, called him "a great baseball player — and a great person." John Spalding, author of *Sacramento Senators and Solons*, thought highly of French and picked him for his "All-Star," "All-Career," and "All-Star," "All-Era" (1920 to 1945) teams. Raymond French died in Alameda, Calif., on April 3, 1978.

"DOLPH" CAMILLI

Babe, TV, Gin

Adolph "Dolph" Louis Camilli was born in San Francisco on April 23, 1907. "Dolph" began playing professional baseball as a first baseman for the San Francisco Seals (Pacific Coast League) in 1926, and later played for the Sacramento Senators from 1929 to 1933. His lifetime PCL batting average was .294. During the 1933 season, Camilli moved to the National League, playing for both

Dolph not only made the last out on Babe Ruth and hit the first televised home run, he was also known to have made a great martini.

the Chicago Cubs and Philadelphia Phillies. From 1938 to 1943 he played for the Brooklyn Dodgers, leading them to the World Series in 1941, and, in the process, winning the 1941 National League Most Valuable Player Award. Camilli finished his big-league career with the Boston Red Sox in 1945. He had a lifetime batting average of .277, a fielding average of .990, and he became a member of the Brooklyn Dodgers Hall of Fame. Camilli was a coach with the Solons in 1947 and again in 1955. His younger brother, Frankie, a boxer who fought as Frankie Campbell, died in the ring in 1930 while fighting Sacramento's heavyweight champ Max Baer. Camilli is a member of the Sacramento Athletic Hall of Fame. He died on Oct. 21, 1997, in San Mateo. Calif.

STANLEY "FRENCHY" BORDAGARAY

Stanley George "Frenchy" Bordagaray was born in Coalinga, Calif., on Jan. 3, 1910. He was the middle child of the seven children of Dominique and Louis Bordagaray, who were among the original settlers of the San Joaquin Valley. Bordagaray grew up in Coalinga and claimed that his father, who had a large family to raise, supplemented his income by bootlegging. The press called Stanley Bordagaray "Frenchy," and he went along with it, but he always pointed out that his father was actually Basque. "Frenchy" attended Fresno State College on an athletic scholarship. There, he was a four-sport letterman and played on the school's first undefeated football team in 1929. His outstanding collegiate performances earned him a tryout with the Sacramento Senators in 1931. The 5-foot-8, 175-pound right-hander was a very colorful player who enjoyed a 17-year professional baseball career.

He played in the outfield for the Sacramento Senators from 1931 to 1934 and batted .335. One of the most interesting stories about him is that he did not come out to his position in right field at the start of the ninth inning in a game against Portland, Ore. When the ball was pitched, the hitter punched it into right field, and by the time the center fielder got to the ball, the batter

had a double. The newspapers blamed "Frenchy," but manager Earl McNeely chewed out the pitcher.

In his book *Baseball's Forgotten Heroes*, author Tony Salin recalls an example of Bordagaray's wit. Once in the heat of an argument, he accidentally spat on an umpire and when fined for it, said, the fine was "more than I expectorated."

"Frenchy" went on to play, primarily in the outfield, for five teams in the major leagues from 1934 to 1945. At the end of the 1934 season, he appeared in 29 games for the Chicago White Sox. From 1935 to 1936 he was one of "dem bums" (a term of endearment for the Brooklyn Dodgers during some of the team's lean years). Once, when Casey Stengel chewed Bordagaray out and fined him for not sliding into third, Bordagaray responded — when he hit a home run — by sliding into first, second, and third and

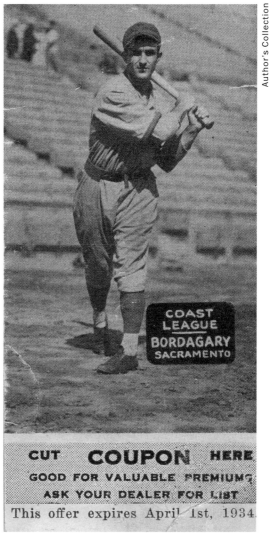

COAST
LEAGUE
BORDAGARY
SACRAMENTO

CUT **COUPON** HERE
GOOD FOR VALUABLE PREMIUMS
ASK YOUR DEALER FOR LIST
This offer expires April 1st, 1934.

making a swan dive onto home plate. Stengel chewed him out again and fined him! Another time when they were playing the Giants and he was playing left field, he went after a fly ball when his hat flew off. He stopped, went back, got his hat, put it on and went and caught the ball.

From 1937 through 1938 Bordagaray roamed the outfield for the St. Louis Cardinals. During spring training with the Cards, he and future Solons player-manager, Pepper Martin, demonstrated sliding techniques.

In the off-season, Bordagaray played the jug in the Cardinal's "Gashouse Gang," known as the "Mississippi Mudcat Band," and it was said that he made more money with the band than he did playing baseball.

In 1939 he joined the Cincinnati Reds' organization, pinch-running for future Solons player and MLB Hall-of-Famer Ernie Lombardi in that year's World Series. In 1940 the Yankees acquired Bordagaray and farmed him out to the Kansas City Blues (American Association), where he was a teammate of Phil Rizzuto's. In 1941 he played 36 games with the World Champion New York Yankees. In later years, family members took turns wearing his World Series championship ring when they accompanied him to ball games.

"Frenchy" finished his major league playing career with the Brooklyn Dodgers, appearing with them from 1942 through 1945. In 1995, he was elected to the Brooklyn Dodgers Hall of Fame.

In 1946 he was the player-manager for the Trois Rivieres Royals baseball club (Canadian-American League). The Trois Rivieres were 72-49 and league champs that year. "Frenchy" led the league with a .363 batting average and was league MVP and coach of the year. In 1947 he was the player-manager for the Greenville Spinners (the South Atlantic League or "Sally League").

In 1943 Bordagaray married, and he and his wife, Victoria, had four children: Christopher, Stanley Jr., Stanna, and Germaine. In the 1950s Bordagaray was a restaurateur and club owner in St. Louis and Kansas City, Mo., and was a developer of 15 cemeteries throughout the Midwest. In 1961 he returned to California, moving his family to Ventura. He worked as a supervisor in the Ventura Sports and Recreation Department, establishing various youth sports programs in the community. During this time he also was active in building local baseball diamonds and referred to himself as a "diamond cutter."

His family said that "Frenchy" had been beaned six times in his career, but he never shied away from a pitch or lost his love of the game. He had a lifetime fielding percentage of .954, and a lifetime major league batting average of .283, but he also had an exceptional pinch-hitting average of .312.

Bordagaray was elected to the Fresno County Sports Hall of Fame in 1962 and the Ventura County Sports Hall of Fame in 1986. He died on April 13, 2001, in Ventura, Calif.

WILBUR ADAMS

Wilbur Adams was a native Sacramentan, an athlete at Sacramento High School and at Stanford University. He became a member of *The Sacramento Bee*'s sports staff during the early 1930s and wrote a column called "Between the Lines." He covered the Solons during the 1930s and '40s and was one of the team's official scorers. Adams is a member of the Sacramento Athletic Hall of Fame.

ANTHONY "TONY" KOESTER

Anthony "Tony" Koester was born in Rock Island, Ill., and was the radio "voice" of the Solons from the late 1930s through the '50s. He graduated from the University of Washington with a degree in journalism, and got his start broadcasting high school sports in Wenatchee, Wash. He went on to broadcast Wenatchee Chief's baseball games in the Western International League.

Koester began broadcasting Solons games in 1938 on KFBK, which was owned by *The Sacramento Bee* and nicknamed the "The Bee Radio Station." He covered most games live in Sacramento, San Francisco and Oakland. He also was well known for recreating road contests from telegraph messages and, for a week each year for several seasons, recreating games in a downtown storefront window — something fans still remember about him.

"Tony" was an award-winning broadcaster who was much loved and described in the 1940s as "a brilliant narrator." He is a member of the Sacramento Athletic Hall of Fame. He died in Oroville, Calif., on Oct. 14, 1996, at the age of 93.

JOHN "PEPPER" MARTIN

John "Pepper" Leonard Roosevelt ("The Wild Horse of the Osage") Martin was born in Temple, Okla., on Feb. 29, 1904. Pepper had a 13-year career with the St. Louis Cardinals starting in 1928. He finished with a lifetime batting average of .298 and appeared on four All-Star teams in the 1930s. He appeared in three World Series, and was a member of the 1931 and 1934 championship teams. Martin managed the Solons in 1941 and 1942, guiding them to the 1942 Pacific Coast League Championship. He died in McAlister, Okla., on March 5, 1965.

WILLIAM "BILL" CONLIN

Resilience

Bill Conlin, legendary sports writer for both the Sacramento Union and the Sacramento Bee used to call Tony Freitas the "gutta percha man." Although probably not understood today, this term was a high compliment in the 1940s. Gutta percha was a natural rubber that was used in golf balls in the 1930s and revolutionized the game of golf. Conlin considered Tony's well used pitching arm to have the same elastic properties that allowed him to pitch so well for so long.

William Richard "Bill" Conlin was born in Sacramento on April 14, 1913. He grew up in Marysville where his interest in sports was fueled by watching the semi-pro Marysville Giants play on Sunday afternoons. He graduated from Stanford University in 1934. Conlin worked for 39 years at the *Sacramento Union* where he was a reporter, sports editor, sports columnist, editor and assistant to the publisher. His tenure at the *Union* was interrupted by a 33-month stint in the U.S. Navy as a junior officer stationed in the Aleutian Islands during World War II.

In 1976 Conlin began working for *The Sacramento Bee*, and retired as a sports editor in 1985. After that, he wrote a nostalgia column that ran every Sunday through 1996. Many Sacramentans fondly remember two of his famous

columns: "It Says Here," and "The Barber Pole: Or, Once Over Lightly." Bill Conlin died in Sacramento on June 9, 1997. After his death, *The Bee's* Bill Vanacore said, "Bill had many tales to tell, in the newsroom and outside of it. And Bill knew his way around the town's bars and eateries."

Author's Collection

DICK EDMONDS

Richard Edmonds was born in 1912 in Sawtelle, Calif. He went to San Jose State College where he was involved in boxing, soccer and tennis. He was a sports reporter for newspapers in Colusa, Pittsburg, Napa, Madera, Bakersfield and San Jose. Edmonds was the *Sacramento Union*'s sports editor from 1942 until he died in 1945.

In Feb. 1944, Edmonds and Yubi Separovich spearheaded a group that headed off the sale and transfer of the Solons to Tacoma. Wash. Along with other businessmen, they incorporated the Sacramento Baseball Association and kept baseball in Sacramento.

Edmonds is buried in the Old City Cemetery across the street from the ballpark. At the beginning of the 1944 season, the name of the park had changed (via a newspaper contest) from Cardinal Field to Doubleday Park. In September of 1945, the name was changed again to Edmonds Field, to honor the man who led the charge to keep baseball in Sacramento. Edmonds died in Sacramento on July 19, 1945.

Author's Collection

YUBI SEPAROVICH

Yubi Separovich was born in Sacramento on June 10, 1915. He was the Solons' general manager in the late 1940s and a driving force in keeping the team in Sacramento after the 1943 season. He worked with sportswriter Dick Edmonds to form the Sacramento Baseball Association, solicit investors and buy the team from the PCL. He is remembered as the man who saved baseball in Sacramento.Separovich later was in the carpet, liquor, and industrial loan businesses, quite active in various civic groups, and an avid golfer. He died in Sacramento on Feb. 11, 2005.

Author's Collection

FRED DAVID

Fred David was born on Oct. 1, 1909, in Rugby, N.D., to Mary and Attas H. David, who came to the United States from Lebanon. David had five brothers and three sisters. In 1921, the family moved to Sacramento where his father was in the vegetable business. David went to Washington Elementary School and began a lifelong love of sports by playing neighborhood basketball and baseball.

David had to go to work at a young age, and during the 1920s he joined his father in the vegetable business in the old Sacramento Public Market at 12th and J streets. The market also housed the Toffanelli Fish Company and Bondi Fruit. David soon tired of the vegetable business, though, and moved on to the Sacramento-based Weinstock-Lubin & Company, where he worked for three years. In 1930, he decided to go into business on his own and moved to San Francisco to get into the candy business in the Crystal Palace Market. It turned out to be a very tough time to get into the business, though, so David returned to Sacramento where he sold radios door-to-door. He married Isabelle Martha Shikany in 1932 and had two children, Gary and Lisa.

The Paperboy
Fred's love of baseball began when he sold newspapers to the Solons who gathered in Charley Doyle's cigar store in the 1920s. He had no idea that years later he would own the ball club.

In the late 1930s, David opened a restaurant, David's Café, at 12th and I streets. He also began David Candy Company, initially operating out of his home at 2020 J St. As his business prospered in the 1940s, he moved into an office with a warehouse at 908 Sixth St. and phased out of David's Café. He bought the property at 12th and I streets and began renting it, later rebuilding and renting to the Continental Trailways busline. In 1962, he purchased the former Fuller Paint building on R Street between 10th and 11th streets. This site currently houses the David Candy Company, the Fox and Goose restaurant, an art gallery and some other small shops.

In 1944 when the St. Louis Cardinals sold the Solons to the Sacramento Baseball Association, David became a stockholder. In 1948 he increased his business interest in the Solons and became a member of the board of directors. In 1951 the major stockholders changed, but David continued on the board and in 1953 became a major stockholder. During this time, the Solons struggled with attendance and finances.

In 1954, after becoming the Solons' president and taking over ownership of Edmonds Field, David led the battle to keep professional baseball alive in Sacramento and, according to *Sacramento Senators and Solons'* author Jack Spalding, vowed that the Solons would stay in Sacramento "until hell freezes over."

But with the coming of the San Francisco Giants in 1958, Sacramento became part of a much smaller market league. In spite of the valiant effort to keep baseball in Sacramento, attendance continued to drop off and financial losses mounted. David sold his interest to a local group, but maintained ownership of Edmonds Field.

From 1961 through 1964 David continued to try to bring a baseball team back to Sacramento and Edmonds Field, but opportunities were minimal and expenses exceeded the income produced by various events. In addition to roller derbies and religious festivals, David sponsored motorcycle races, which because of the noise, lasted only through 1961. In 1964, the property was sold to a grocery-store chain and the stadium was torn down.

David has tremendous memories of his days in baseball. Tony Freitas and Joe Marty were two of his favorite players, and his favorite manager was Tommy Heath.

Today, David enjoys operating the David Candy Company, which wholesales candy, gum and cigarettes, and employs 11.

ERNIE LOMBARDI

Ernesto "Ernie" Natali (Schnozz or Bocci) Lombardi was born in Oakland, Calif., on April 6, 1908. He was catcher for the Oakland Oaks (Pacific Coast League) from 1926 to 1930. Lombardi had 17 outstanding seasons in the National League. He broke in with Brooklyn in 1931, but spent most of his career with the Cincinnati Reds from 1932 to 1941. In 1942 Lombardi played for the Boston Braves, and from 1943 to 1947 he was with the New York Giants. His MLB lifetime batting average was .306, and he won the league batting crowns in 1938 and 1942. He appeared in two World Series with

Cincinnati (in 1939 and 1940) with the Reds winning the championship in 1940. He made eight National League All-Star teams between 1936 and 1945 and was the league MVP in 1938. Lombardi played for the Solons in 1948 and had a lifetime PCL batting average of .349. He was elected to the MLB Hall of Fame in 1986 and to the PCL Hall of Fame in 2003. He died in Santa Cruz, Calif. on Sept. 26, 1977.

LELAND "LEE" SUSMAN

Leland "Lee" Stanford Susman was born in San Francisco on July 27, 1917. His cartoon artwork graced most of the Solons' program covers in the 1950s, and his whimsical athletic Capitol dome stands out as one of the all-time great graphic features of Sacramento professional baseball. Susman grew up in San Francisco, attending Galileo High School, the California School of Fine Arts, and the College of Advertising Fine Arts. He grew up a self-described "sports nut" and in about 1937, he began working for a small advertising agency. In

1939, he won a competition to draw a comic strip for the *San Francisco Call-Bulletin*. In 1940 he had an opportunity to work with renowned cartoonist Jimmy Hatlo, but World War II intervened. In January 1946, after five years in the Navy during World War II, the *Oakland Tribune* hired Susman as a sports cartoonist. In 1946 he originated "The Lil' Acorn," the Oakland Oaks' mascot, and later in the early 1950s, he created the Solons' dome. He retired in 1983, and still watches baseball and enjoys PCL reunions.

1951

Lee Susman

TO FRIEND, ALAN O'CONNOR WITH ALL
BEST WISHS. From *Lee Susman* 8/10/02

Doug McWilliams Collection

"BILLY" RAIMONDI

William Louis "Billy" Raimondi was born in San Francisco on Dec. 1, 1913, and grew up in Oakland. The 5-foot-10, 165-pound right-hander had a stellar 21-year career as a catcher in the Pacific Coast League, primarily with the Oakland Oaks.

Raimondi was a student and a two-time all-city catcher at Oakland's McClymonds High School. In 1931, while he was still in school, he signed with the Oakland Oaks. He played in Phoenix and Bisbee, Ariz., before joining the Oaks in 1932.

"Billy" was a solid backstop for the Oaks from 1933 through 1935, but missed the entire 1936 season due to an arm injury during spring training. He caught in most of the Oaks games from 1937 through 1948. Raimondi also managed the Oaks for much of the second half of the 1945 season when "Dolph" Camilli stepped down. When Casey Stengel replaced Raimondi as manager in 1946, Raimondi stayed with the team and became one of Stengel's "Nine Old Men" — who went on to win the 1948 PCL championship.

Partway through the 1949 season, the Oaks traded Raimondi to the Solons. In 1950 he caught in 110 games for them. From 1951 through 1953, he played for the Los Angeles Angels but was used sparingly and retired after that season. Three of his brothers also played for the Oaks.

Raimondi was a regular player in 17 of his 21 seasons, appearing in 2,186 games with a lifetime batting average of .274. He is a particular favorite of Oaks' historian Bill Shubb, who says Raimondi played more seasons in the PCL than any other field player in the history of the league, and points out he was an All-Star 16 times in his 21 seasons in the PCL.

"RAY" DANDRIDGE

Raymond "Ray" Emmitt Dandridge was born in Richmond, Va., on Aug. 31, 1913. The 5-foot-7, 170-pound right-hander was one of the best defensive third basemen in baseball history and consistently batted above .300.

Dandridge played in the Negro Leagues in the 1930s and '40s primarily for the Newark Eagles. In 1933 he played for the Detroit Stars, the Nashville Elite Giants, and the Newark Dodgers, and returned to the Dodgers for 1934 and 1935. From 1936 through 1939, in 1942 and again in 1944, he was with the Newark Eagles. In 1949 he was with the New York Cubans. He also spent eight summers in the Mexican League and 11 winters in the Cuban Winter League. Once the color barrier fell, Dandridge played four years with the Minneapolis Millers, a Giants' affiliate, where he was the American Association's MVP in 1950 at the age of 37! He spent part of the 1953 season with the Solons. Dandridge was elected to the Hall of Fame in 1987. He died in Palm Bay, Fla., on Feb. 12, 1994.

"WALT" FITZPATRICK

Walter Fitzpatrick was born in Pueblo, Colo., on Sept. 28, 1934, to Elise and John Wallace Fitzpatrick. He grew up in Napa and in the 1940s frequently visited the Oakland Oaks' spring training and volunteered to get the balls "game ready" by rubbing them with mud. He eventually worked his way up to becoming one of the Sunday batboys during 1947 and 1948. He fondly remembers getting autographs from his heroes — Dario Lodigani, George Metkovich and Billy Raimondi.

Fitzpatrick's father, John Wallace Fitzpatrick, played for Pueblo (Colo.) on the Washington Senators' farm system. He named "Walt" after the legendary Walter Johnson.

In the late 1920s, the senior Fitzpatrick managed a team in Centerville, Iowa, that had an outfielder he thought looked and played like Joe Jackson. In fact, it was Joe Jackson. Since Jackson had been banished from baseball after the 1919 "Black Sox" scandal, this brush with infamy got John Wallace Fitzpatrick suspended from baseball. When his father died in 1948, Fitzpatrick and his mother moved to Sacramento where he began playing outfield for Kelly's Feed and Fuel in Sacramento's 125-pound league, which was held in McKinley Park. In 1949 Fitzpatrick went to Concordia College (a combination high school and junior college) in Oakland. He played baseball at Concordia from 1949 through 1953. Because Oakland Oaks' coaches often helped Concordia's team, Fitzpatrick benefited from the experiences of pros such as Max Carey, Charlie Dressen and Mel Ott.

In 1954 Fitzpatrick returned to Sacramento and played ball for Sacramento Junior College (now Sacramento City College), batting .417. He also had the good fortune to attend the St. Louis Cardinals' tryout camp later that year. Baseball scout Bill Avila noticed him, and Fitzpatrick went to spring training with the Solons in 1955. He did not make the roster, but spent most of the season with the "Junior Solons" (a development team).

Fitzpatrick married in 1959 and had two children: Michael and Jennifer. After he left baseball, he took advanced studies in aeronautics and worked at Aerojet General Corporation. While there, he worked with Wernher von Braun, who has been called one of the most important rocket developers between 1930 and 1970. When Aerojet downsized, Fitzpatrick went into the justice system and now has his own evidence display company, Amicus Curiae Design.

"BOB" LEMON

Robert "Bob" Granville Lemon was born on Sept. 22, 1920, in San Bernardino, Calif. The 6-foot, 185-pounder batted left and threw right. He played 15 years — 13 as a pitcher — with the Cleveland Indians in the 1940s and '50s. He was a four-time All-Star in 1948, 1949, 1950 and 1951. He had seven 20-win seasons. Only three other American League pitchers had accomplished that at that time: Lefty Grove, Walter Johnson and Ed Plank, all in the Hall of Fame. Lemon was a key factor for Cleveland in 1948 when they beat the Boston

Braves in the World Series and in the 1954 pennant drive, posting records of 20-14 and 23-7, respectively. Lemon played in two World Series for the Indians. His lifetime pitching record was 207 wins with 128 losses with an earned run average of 3.23. He led the league in wins in 1950 with 23, in 1954 with 23 and in 1955 with 18. Lemon's fellow pitchers with Cleveland were Bob Feller and Early Winn, and he was teammates with Wally Westlake for four years.

After he retired as a player following the 1958 season, Lemon served as a scout and coach for the Indians. He managed Hawaii's PCL Islanders in 1964, and Seattle's PCL ball club in 1965 and 1966. Later Lemon coached for the Philadelphia Phillies, California Angels and the Kansas City Royals. In 1969 he managed the Vancouver, British Columbia, ball club. He was named manager of the Kansas City Royals in 1970 and held that post through the 1972 season. In 1973 he scouted for the Royals.

Lemon managed the Solons for the 1974 season, and one of the team's programs included these comments. "Being a former pitcher I've always emphasized pitching and defense," he said. "Hughes Stadium could persuade me to change some of my strategy. We'll have some very exciting baseball with plenty of big innings. The last out will really count in this park."

In 1975 Lemon served as a scout for the Atlanta Braves and finished the season as the manager of the Braves' Richmond ball club (International League).

In 1976 he became the pitching coach for the New York Yankees, and in 1978 he managed the Yankees to the World Series Championship. He was inducted into the MLB Hall of Fame in 1976 along with Robin Roberts. Lemon also portrayed future Hall-of-Fame pitcher Jesse Haines in the 1952 film, *The Winning Team*, which starred the future president of the United States, Ronald Reagan, as Hall-of-Fame pitcher Grover Cleveland Alexander. Lemon died on Jan. 11, 2000, in Long Beach, Calif.

John Moist Collection

ABOUT THE AUTHOR

Alan O'Connor grew up in Sacramento, going to school with many children of Solons players. He graduated from McClatchy High School and the University of California, Davis. He has always had an interest in history, particularly the history of California and Sacramento.

O'Connor spent lots of happy days attending Solons games at Edmonds Field. He is a member of the Society for American Baseball Research (SABR) and the Pacific Coast League Historical Society. He is also a member of the board of directors of the Sacramento County Historical Society, and has provided input to the Solons website at http://members.tripod.com/~acorns/solons.

For several years O'Connor has displayed the *History of Sacramento Professional Baseball 1886-1976* in the Sacramento Room of the Central Branch of the Sacramento Public Library, as well as in the History Center at the Sacramento Discovery Museum and in many Sacramento Public Library branches. He was the historian for the Golden Empire Council of the Boy Scouts of America throughout the 1980s and '90s, and was principal author of *The History of the Golden Empire Council, BSA.* He has also written numerous journal articles about Scouting history, and has spent the last few decades producing historical displays at Scouting and community events.

O'Connor has worked at the California Department of Aging (CDA) since the 1980s, and is currently a health program specialist with the Multipurpose Senior Services Program (MSSP), which provides care management and other services that keep frail seniors in their communities and out of nursing facilities.

Left: inside label of teens vintage cap.

VISITORS		1	2	3	4	5	6	7	8	9	10	AB	R	H	SH	PO	A	E

1 REESE, Coach
2 BECQUER, Inf.
3 BAILEY, C.
9 HERRERA, P.
10 CARMICHAEL, P.
12 ATLWARD, C.
13 DICKEY, P.
15 FABER, Of.
16 FEDEROFF, Inf.
17 RAPP, Inf.
18 SISLER, Inf.
19 MERSON, Inf.
20 FRAUTT, P.
21 BISHOP, P.
22 MADDERN, Of.
24 RIDZIK, P.
25 KAZAK, Of.
26 THOMASON, P.
27 JABLONSKI, Of.
28 PETERSON, Inf.
29 KERRIGAN, P.
30 ELLIOTT, Mgr.
37 Mc LISH, P.

SACRAMENTO		1	2	3	4	5	6	7	8	9	10	AB	R	H	SH	PO	A	E
SS	1																	
2B	2																	
CF	12																	
1B	3																	
3B	3																	
LF	5																	
RF	10																	
C	14																	
P																		

1 MYERS, Inf.
2 STREETER, Inf.
3 JONES V., Inf.
4 PIERETTI, P.
5 MIERKOWICZ, Of.
6 BRIGHT, Inf.
7 CAMILLI, Coach
8 HESLET, Of.
9 TOBIN, Of.
10 CRAWFORD, Of.
11 PRIETAS, Mgr.
13 GLAVIANO, Of.
15 BRIGGS, P.
16 JONES R., P.
17 WATKINS, P.
18 DALEY, P.
19 SHEELY, C.
20 CANDINI, P.
22 OLSENBAUGH, P.
23 HEIST, Of.
24 JOHNSON, P.
26 HARRIST, P.

BIBLIOGRAPHY

Books and articles

Armour, Mark. *Rain Check: Baseball in the Pacific Northwest.* Cleveland, Ohio: The Society for American Baseball Research, Inc., 2006.

Bauer, Carlos. *The Coast League Cyclopedia: An encyclopedia of the old Pacific Coast League, 1903-57.* Vols. 1-3. San Diego, Calif.: Baseball Press Books, 2003.

Dobbins, Dick and Jon Twichell. *Nuggets on the Diamond: Professional Baseball in the Bay Area from the Gold Rush to the Present.* San Francisco, Calif.: Woodford Press, 1994.

Dobbins, Dick. *The Grand Minor League.* Emeryville, Calif.: Woodford Press, 1999.

Lange, Fred W. *History of Baseball in California and Pacific Coast Leagues, 1847-1938; Memories and Musings of an Old time Baseball Player.* Oakland, Calif.: Privately published, 1938.

O'Neal, Bill. *The Pacific Coast League, 1903-1988.* Austin, Texas: Eakin Publications, 1990.

Pendleton, Frances F. *Friendly Trials of Skill,* Sacramento, Calif.: Sacramento County Historical Society, 1988.

Ritter, Lawrence S. *The Glory of Their Times: The Story of Baseball Told By the Men Who Played It.* New York, N.Y.: William Morrow and Company, Inc., 1992.

Salin, Tony. *Baseball's Forgotten Heroes: One Man's Search for the Game's Most Interesting Overlooked Players.* Chicago, Ill.: Masters Press, 1999.

Spalding, John E. *Pacific Coast League Stars: Ninety Who Made it in the*

t: 1955 team line-up (Author's collection).

Majors, 1903-1957. Vol. 1, 1994; Vol. 2; Privately published, 1997.

Spalding, John E. *Always on Sunday.* Manhattan, Kan.: Ag Press, 1992.

Spalding, John E. *Sacramento's Senators and Solons: Baseball in California's Capital, 1886 to 1976.* Manhattan, Kan.: Ag Press, 1995.

Wells, Donald R. *The Race for the Governor's Cup.* Jefferson, N.C.: McFarland & Company, Inc., Publishers, 2000.

Zervos, Diamantis. *Baseball's Golden Greeks.* Canton, Mass.: Aegean Books International, 1998.

Zingg, Paul J. and Mark D. Medeiros. *Runs, Hits and an Era — 1903-1958.* Urbana, Ill.: University of Illinois Press, 1994.

Newspapers

The *Alameda Times-Star,* April 4, 1978

The *Sacramento Bee,* 1886-1976

The *Sacramento Union,* 1886-1976

The *Wenatchee Daily World,* 1946

The *Woodland Daily Democrat,* Oct. 9, 1940

Record books

The Baseball Encyclopedia. New York, N.Y.: Macmillan Publishing Company, 1990.

Pacific Coast League Record Book, 1903-1940.

Websites

Mike McCann's Minor League Baseball History; geocities.com/big_bunko.

Pacific Coast League; minorleaguebaseball.com.

Sacramento Solons; sacramentosolons.com.

March 29, 30, 31-31—Los Angeles at Sacramento; Seattle at San Francisco; Portland at Hollywood; Oakland at San Diego.

April 2, 3, 4, 5, 6, 7-7—Hollywood at Sacramento; Portland at Oakland; Seattle at Los Angeles; San Francisco at San Diego.

April 9, 10, 11, 12, 13, 14-14—Oakland at Sacramento; Portland at San Francisco; Seattle at Hollywood; Los Angeles at San Diego.

April 16, 17, 18, 19, 20, 21-21—Sacramento at Los Angeles; San Diego at Seattle; Hollywood at Portland; San Francisco at Oakland.

April 23, 24, 25, 26, 27, 28-28—Sacramento at San Francisco; Hollywood at Seattle; San Diego at Portland; Oakland at Los Angeles.

April 30, May 1, 2, 3, 4, 5-5—San Diego at Sacramento; Seattle at Portland; Los Angeles at San Francisco; Oakland at Hollywood.

May 7, 8, 9, 10, 11, 12-12—San Francisco at Sacramento; Seattle at Oakland; Portland at Los Angeles; Hollywood at San Diego.

May 14, 15, 16, 17, 18, 19-19—Sacramento at San Diego; Portland at Seattle; Hollywood at Oakland; San Francisco at Los Angeles.

May 21, 22, 23, 24, 25, 26-26—Sacramento at Seattle; Oakland at Portland; San Diego at San Francisco; Los Angeles at Hollywood.

May 28, 29, 30-30—Sacramento at Portland; Oakland at Seattle; Hollywood at San Francisco; San Diego at Los Angeles.

May 31, June 1, 2-2—Seattle at Sacramento; Los Angeles at Oakland; San Francisco at Hollywood; Portland at San Diego.

June 4, 5, 6, 7, 8, 9-9—Portland at Sacramento; Oakland at San Francisco; Hollywood at Los Angeles; Seattle at San Diego.

June 11, 12, 13, 14, 15, 16-16—Sacramento at Oakland; Los Angeles at Seattle; San Francisco at Portland; San Diego at Hollywood.

June 18, 19, 20—Sacramento at Hollywood; San Francisco at Seattle; Los Angeles at Portland; San Diego at Oakland.

June 21, 22, 23-23—Seattle at Sacramento; Hollywood at San Francisco; Oakland at Los Angeles; Portland at San Diego.

June 25, 26, 27, 28, 29, 30-30—Hollywood at Sacramento; Seattle at Oakland; Portland at Los Angeles; San Francisco at San Diego.

July 2, 3, 4-4, 5, 6, 7-7—Sacramento at Seattle; Oakland at Portland; Los Angeles at San Francisco; San Diego at Hollywood.

July 9, 10, 11, 12, 13, 14-14—Sacramento at Portland; Oakland at Seattle; San Diego at San Francisco; Hollywood at Los Angeles.

July 16, 17, 18, 19, 20, 21-21—San Diego at Sacramento; Seattle at Portland; Los Angeles at Oakland; San Francisco at Hollywood.

July 23, 24, 25, 26, 27, 28-28—San Francisco at Sacramento; Portland at Oakland; Seattle at Los Angeles; Hollywood at San Diego.

July 30, 31, August 1, 2, 3, 4-4—Sacramento at San Diego; Portland at Seattle; Oakland at San Francisco; Los Angeles at Hollywood.

August 6, 7, 8, 9, 10, 11-11—Sacramento at Los Angeles; San Francisco at Seattle; Hollywood at Portland; San Diego at Oakland.

August 13, 14, 15, 16, 17, 18-18—Oakland at Sacramento; Portland at San Francisco; Seattle at Hollywood; Los Angeles at San Diego.

August 20, 21, 22, 23, 24, 25-25—Portland at Sacramento; Hollywood at Oakland; San Francisco at Los Angeles; Seattle at San Diego.

August 27, 28, 29, 30, 31, September 1-1—Sacramento at Hollywood; Los Angeles at Seattle; San Diego at Portland; San Francisco at Oakland.

September 2-2, 3, 4, 5, 6, 7, 8-8—Sacramento at San Francisco; San Diego at Seattle; Oakland at Hollywood; Los Angeles at Portland.

September 10, 11, 12, 13, 14, 15-15—Los Angeles at Sacramento; Seattle at San Francisco; Portland at Hollywood; Oakland at San Diego.

September 17, 18, 19, 20, 21, 22-22—Sacramento at Oakland; Hollywood at Seattle; San Francisco at Portland; San Diego at Los Angeles.

Dan Murray, 1919 Senators (Author's Collection)

INDEX

John Bromely, 1919 Senators (Author's Collection)